7⁵⁰

SC
RIC

G.W. Dickson

# THE SCROLLS
# FROM THE DEAD SEA

*Other books by*

EDMUND WILSON

I THOUGHT OF DAISY

CLASSICS AND COMMERCIALS

MEMOIRS OF HECATE COUNTY

TO THE FINLAND STATION

THE SHORES OF LIGHT

AXEL'S CASTLE

POET'S FAREWELL

THE AMERICAN JITTERS

TRAVELS IN TWO DEMOCRACIES

THE TRIPLE THINKERS

THE SHOCK OF RECOGNITION

EUROPE WITHOUT BAEDEKER

NOTE-BOOKS OF NIGHT

THE WOUND AND THE BOW

FIVE PLAYS

# The Scrolls
# from the
# Dead Sea

## EDMUND WILSON

W. H. ALLEN
LONDON
1955

*Printed in England by the Ditchling Press Ltd, Ditchling, Sussex, for the publishers,*
*W. H. Allen & Co., Ltd, Essex Street, London, W.C.2*

# Contents

# ACKNOWLEDGEMENTS

This essay, in a somewhat abridged form, first appeared in the *New Yorker* magazine. I am indebted to that periodical for making possible my trip to Palestine, and to its editors and checking department for the careful attention they gave the text.

I should also thank the Metropolitan Mar Athanasius Yeshue Samuel, Père Roland de Vaux of the Ecole Biblique in Old Jerusalem, Dr. James Muilenberg of the Union Theological Seminary, and Dr. W. F. Albright of Johns Hopkins for reading all or part of the manuscript and giving me the benefit of their criticisms and corrections, as well as for assistance of other kinds. I also owe a special debt to Mr. Stewart Perowne of Jerusalem, who arranged my expedition to the Dead Sea.

# I

## *The Metropolitan Samuel*

AT SOME POINT rather early in the spring of 1947, a
Bedouin boy called Muhammed the Wolf was mind-
ing some goats near a cliff on the western shore of the
Dead Sea. Climbing up after one that had strayed,
he noticed a cave that he had not seen before, and
he idly threw a stone into it. There was an unfamiliar
sound of breakage. The boy was frightened and ran
away. But he later came back with another boy, and
together they explored the cave. Inside were several
tall clay jars, among fragments of other jars. When
they took off the bowl-like lids, a very bad smell
arose, which came from dark oblong lumps that
were found inside all the jars. When they got these
lumps out of the cave, they saw they were wrapped
up in lengths of linen and coated with a black layer
of what seemed to be pitch or wax. They unrolled
them and found long manuscripts, inscribed in

7

parallel columns on thin sheets that had been sewn together. Though these manuscripts had faded and crumbled in places, they were in general remarkably clear. The character, they saw, was not Arabic. They wondered at the scrolls and kept them, carrying them along when they moved.

These Bedouin boys belonged to a party of contrabanders, who had been smuggling their goats and other goods out of Transjordan into Palestine. They had detoured so far to the south in order to circumvent the Jordan bridge, which the customs officers guarded with guns, and had floated their commodities across the stream. They were now on their way to Bethlehem to sell their stuff in the black market, and they had come to the Dead Sea in order to stock up with water at the spring of Ain Feshkha, the only fresh water to be found for miles in that dry, hot and desolate region. They were quite safe from discovery there: it was a locality that had no attractions, to which nobody ever came. In Bethlehem, they sold their contraband, and showed their scrolls to the merchant who was buying it. He did not know what they were and refused to pay the twenty pounds they asked for them; so they took them to another merchant, from whom they always bought their supplies. Being a Syrian, he thought that the language might be ancient Syriac, and he sent word by another Syrian to the Syrian Metropolitan at the Monastery of St Mark in Old Jerusalem.

The Metropolitan, Mar Athanasius Yeshue Samuel, expressed a decided interest. He knew that nobody since the first Christian centuries had lived anywhere near Ain Feshkha, and he had been struck by the visitors' telling him that the scrolls were "wrapped up like mummies." When one was brought to him at the monastery, he broke off a bit and burned it, and could smell that it was leather or parchment. He recognized the language as Hebrew, but was not a Hebrew scholar and could not make out what the manuscript was. He sent word that he would buy the scrolls, but in the meantime the Bedouins were off again on another expedition. Several weeks passed. It was July before one of the Syrians called up to tell the Metropolitan that he and the Bedouins would bring him the scrolls. The Metropolitan expected them all morning, and finally went to lunch, and it was then that the visitors arrived. They were turned away at the door, and the priest who had refused to receive them came to the Metropolitan and told him that some tough-looking Arabs had appeared with some dirty old rolls, and that, seeing that these were written not in Syriac but in Hebrew, he had sent the Arabs to a Jewish school. The Metropolitan at once got in touch with the Syrian who had brought the Bedouins and learned with annoyance that these latter, turned away, had shown the scrolls to a Jewish merchant, whom they met at the Jaffa Gate. This merchant had offered them what they thought a good

9

price, but explained that, in order to collect it, they must come to his office in the Jaffa Road in the predominantly Jewish New City.

Now, Jerusalem, by the summer of '47, was already sharply divided between the Arabs and the Jews. The British, in their effort to propitiate the Arabs and to keep them out of the hands of Russia, had prevented refugees from Europe from landing in Palestine ports, and this had imposed on the emigrants much hardship and even caused a large number of deaths. The Jews, in reprisal for this, had organized a terrorist group, which had been murdering British soldiers, and the British had been hanging these terrorists. The Jews had retaliated with bombs and mines, leaving a hangman's noose on the scene of each assassination. The British had then kidnapped a sixteen-year-old boy, who was supposed to be a member of the Stern group. The Jews believed him to have been tortured and killed: his body was never found; and the terrorists blew a hole in the jail where the British had been locking up political prisoners. Some of the men who had done this were caught and hanged, and the Jews hanged two British sergeants and wired one of the bodies with a booby-trap. At the time when the scrolls were thus offered for sale, the Jewish parts of Jerusalem had been put under martial law; and, in consequence, the Syrian merchant, who wanted to have the scrolls go to the monastery, had no difficulty in convincing the Bedouins that the Jewish merchant was planning to trap them—that, once off base in the Jaffa Road, they would be robbed of their property and put in jail; and he mentioned the Palestinian law that newly discovered antiquities must immediately be reported to the government. He even induced the Bedouins to leave five of the scrolls in his shop, and eventually to take them to the monastery, where the Metropolitan purchased them, along with a few fragments, for a price which has never been made public but which is rumoured to have been fifty pounds.

The Metropolitan Samuel has sometimes been charged with slyness in his handling of the Dead Sea scrolls; but if occasionally he has exercised guile, I believe that it has been only such wariness in the matter of not showing one's hand as is quite conventional in the Middle East—a minimum routine requirement in a land where all business transactions are based on a convention of bargaining. I should say, in fact, that, far from having got himself into trouble by trying to be too clever, the Metropolitan has been handicapped by innocence. Not knowing the Western world, it was long, as will later appear, before he was able to profit in any degree proportionate to the value of his unique acquisitions; and he deserves immense credit, one cannot but feel —especially if one takes into account the chapter of ineptitude that follows—for having had the good sense to recognize that hitherto unknown manuscripts from the uninhabited region of the Dead Sea would be likely to prove of interest, and for persisting, in the teeth of discouragement, in sticking by this conviction. With his black and abundant beard, his large round liquid brown eyes, in his onion-shaped black satin mitre, his black robes with their big sleeves and the great cross of gold and the ikon of the Virgin that hang about his neck on chains, the Metropolitan—with not too much priestly fleshiness and pallor—is a notably handsome man, who would recall an Assyrian bas-relief if his expression were not gentle instead of fierce. In demeanour, he is dignified, simple and calm, with a touch perhaps of something childlike. He is not at all an "intellectual," has no special scholarly interests, but is much devoted to his church, the Syrian Jacobite Church, which long antedates the Greek and boasts that its line comes direct from the Holy See of Antioch founded by Peter, and that it ruled at one time the whole Christian East. This is one of the five churches permanently represented in the Church of the Holy Sepulchre, and the Monastery of St. Mark is supposed to stand on the site of the house where the Last Supper occurred.

The first thing the Metropolitan Samuel did when he had bought the Hebrew manuscripts was to send one of his priests with the merchant to check up on the story of the cave. The cave was found in the place that the Bedouins had indicated, and in it were found the jars, fragments of the linen wrappings and scraps of the scrolls themselves. The two men spent a night in the cavern, stifling in the terrible heat—it was now the second week of August —and, having brought no provisions but melons, they decided they could not stay longer. They did not even manage to bring away, as at first they had hoped to do, one of the big clay jars. (The Bedouins, however, had taken two and had been using them to carry water.) The problem was now to find out what the manuscripts were and how old they were. The Metropolitan Samuel consulted a Syrian he knew in the Palestine Department of Antiquities, and a French priest at the Dominican Ecole Biblique, a centre of archaeological research in Old Jerusalem.

The outsider cannot but be struck by the frequent reluctance of the learned world to recognize important discoveries. In connection with the failure of scholars first to recognize, then to acknowledge, the antiquity of the Dead Sea scrolls, Professor W. F. Albright of Johns Hopkins has pointed out that "the discovery of Pompeii and Herculaneum was in its time relegated to the realm of fiction by outstanding personages, that some archaeologists and many more philologians refused to accept the stratigraphical results of Schliemann and Dörpfeld for decades after the beginning of the excavations of Hissarlik [ancient Troy], and that the decipherment of cuneiform was not accepted by all informed students of antiquity until well after the end of the nineteenth century." There have been forgeries and hoaxes, of course: the false books of Livy, the supplement to Petronius; and the scholar must be on his guard against innocently swallowing such products. Yet there is also at work here the natural instinct to simplify one's scholarly problems by establishing a closed field. One likes to feel that one has seen all the evidence. One has mastered it and worked out one's theories; and it is very upsetting—especially, if one suffers from imaginative limitations—to have to be obliged to deal with new material. There are still doubts expressed in some quarters as to the genuineness of the great Russian medieval poem, *The Expedition of Igor*. The only manuscript of this was discovered in the eighteenth century, and this original, although it had been copied, was burned in the Moscow fire of 1812. Yet the case against it is really based on the argument that there is nothing else like it, and the argument for its authenticity was definitively put by Pushkin when he declared that, in the eighteenth century, there existed no known Russian writer who was gifted and learned enough to have perpetrated so brilliant a hoax. How much stronger, then, both for and against, are the arguments in respect to the scrolls! How much more improbable, on the one hand, the finding of Biblical manuscripts that antedate those that were known! How even more improbable that anyone should attempt so elaborate a fraud!

In order to understand the importance of the Dead Sea manuscripts and the stubborn incredulity

of scholars, one has to realize that, except for a fragment or two, our earliest text of the Hebrew Bible—
the so-called Masoretic text—is no more ancient
than the ninth century of the Christian era; and
that, before that, our main versions of Scripture are
the Alexandrian Septuagint, a translation into
Greek which is supposed to have been begun somewhere in the third pre-Christian century and not
finished till two hundred years later, and St.
Jerome's Latin Vulgate, made in the fourth century.
All our knowledge of the word of the Bible has been
based on these two translations and this very late
Hebrew text (helped out with a Samaritan Pentateuch and some excerpts in early Aramaic versions).
It took some courage to face new materials where
none had been imagined to exist. "In none of the
similar episodes of the past two centuries . . ." continues Professor Albright, "has there been such a
wide refusal on the part of scholars to accept clear-
cut evidence." The first experts consulted by the
Metropolitan Samuel gave him no encouragement
whatever. The two ablest archaeologists then in that
part of the world were apparently Mr. G. Lankester
Harding of the Department of Antiquities of Transjordan and Père Roland de Vaux of the Ecole
Biblique; but the latter at the moment was away in
Paris, and to the former the Metropolitan did not
succeed in gaining access. The people whom he did
see at these institutions told him that the thing was
unheard of: the manuscripts could not be old. No

effort seems even to have been made to read them
till the Metropolitan showed them to a Father van
der Ploeg, a visiting Dutch scholar at the Ecole
Biblique, who identified one of the scrolls as Isaiah,
but was discouraged by the scholars of the school
from pursuing the matter further.

The Metropolitan now took the scrolls to the
Syrian Patriarch of Antioch, who thought they
could not be more than three centuries old, but
suggested his consulting the professor of Hebrew at
the American University in Beirut. The Metropolitan went to Beirut but found the professor away on
vacation. He decided to study the problem himself,
and, coming back to Jerusalem, he got his friend
from the Department of Antiquities to supply him
with some books on the Hebrew alphabet. The
Syrian archaeologist assured him that he was wast-
ing his time, that the scrolls were "not worth a
shilling"; but the Syrian brought to the monastery
a Jew from the New City, a Mr. Tovia Wechsler,
who was something of a Hebrew scholar. This visit
of Mr. Wechsler, according to the Metropolitan's
account, occurred toward the end of September.
Mr. Wechsler, however, remembers it as having
taken place already—in July—and his statement
about it is also at variance with what was later
known definitely about the scrolls. He, too, was
unable to believe they were as old as the Metropolitan hoped. Mr. Wechsler pointed at the table
on which the manuscripts had been laid—about

this he and the Metropolitan are agreed—and declared, "If that table were a box, and you filled it
with pound notes, you couldn't even manage the
value of the scrolls, if they are two thousand years
old, as you say." He did not credit the story of their
having been found in a cave by the Dead Sea. He
noticed, in examining one of them, that corrections
written in the margins and fillings-out of the columns at the bottoms, where the text was becoming
obliterated, had been made in an ink that contrasted
by its clearness with the ink of the original copyist,
and he drew the inference from this that the scroll
"had been in use by a very poor community for a
considerable time and had only recently been
abandoned." He jumped to the conclusion that the
manuscripts had been stolen from a Palestine synagogue at the time of the anti-Jewish Arab riots of
1929. He recognized a text of Isaiah and observed
that it differed slightly from the Masoretic text. The
second of the rolls that he examined he believed to
be a Haftaroth scroll—that is, a selection from the
Prophets of lessons to be read in synagogues. But no
Haftaroth have ever turned up among the known
Dead Sea scrolls, and the Metropolitan says that
what Wechsler must have taken for a Haftaroth
scroll was a manuscript of the Torah (the Pentateuch) which was shown him on the same visit but
which had nothing to do with the Dead Sea lot.
Among these, as was afterwards found, were three
non-Biblical books which had never been seen

before, and others think that Mr. Wechsler must hastily have taken one of these for a modern synagogue scroll. To this theory Wechsler replies that it reminds him "of the story about the man who related that he had seen a camel, and after having circumstantially described the animal, was asked by someone in his audience, 'Maybe you saw a cat?' " The incident remains rather obscure. When the matter was later looked into by the American School of Oriental Research, the only Hebrew manuscript the searchers found in the library of the monastery was a relatively modern Torah.

"Needless to say I felt discouraged", the Metropolitan writes, "but somehow I still felt they were wrong." One may at first find it surprising that a man of such importance in Jerusalem—the equivalent of a Western archbishop—should have taken so long a time to discover the competent authorities, who were right there ready to hand; but one is often surprised in Jerusalem at the lack of knowledge and interest shown by the various groups in one another's affairs. In the published discussion of the scrolls one finds, for example, that the Metropolitan Samuel is sometimes referred to as "the Patriarch"; and, in talking with scholars in the New City, on a recent visit to Israel, I was astonished by their vagueness about him: some imagined him to be still in his monastery, though he had left it in 1948. It will be noticed that the Metropolitan, in his efforts to deal with the scrolls, almost always has recourse to other Syrians. In the Middle East, it seems, your church is your social world, and you know little, apparently, of any other. Even in the United States, the congregations of the four different Syrian churches mix little with one another; and an American is sometimes puzzled, in crossing some frontier in the Middle East, to be asked for his "nationality" when he has already registered his American citizenship: "nationality", he learns, means "religion." At any rate, it seems to have been only by chance that the Metropolitan Samuel did finally get in touch with an institution that could help him, and, even then, the contact had no results. It happened that a Jewish doctor called at the Monastery to inquire about renting a building that was a part of the church's property. The Metropolitan took the opportunity to ask him about the scrolls. This visitor did the obvious thing: he called up President Magnes of the Hebrew University. Dr. Magnes, a few weeks later, sent two men from the University library. They said that they would have to consult an authority on these subjects and asked to photograph a few columns of one of the manuscripts. The Metropolitan gave his consent, but the librarians never came back. On the same afternoon, also summoned by the doctor, a Jewish antiquity dealer arrived at the monastery. He recommended that pieces of the scrolls be sent to certain dealers in Europe and the United States. "This," says the Metropolitan Samuel, "I declined to do."

It is not clear whether the failure of the men from the library to come back, as they promised, to the monastery was due to the troubled conditions or to the absence of E. L. Sukenik, the University's head archaeologist. In any case, Professor Sukenik returned at the end of November, and was told by a Jerusalem antiquity dealer (not the one who had visited the monastery) that some manuscripts from a cave on the Dead Sea were in the hands of a dealer in Bethlehem. This dealer was the buyer of contraband to whom the Bedouins had first brought the scrolls. He had got wind of their having some value and had bought up the remaining manuscripts. These were the three other scrolls that the Metropolitan Samuel had not had a chance to buy.

What followed was recorded by Sukenik in his diary:

"November 25, 1947: Today I met X [antiquity dealer]. A Hebrew book has been discovered in a jar. He showed me a fragment written on parchment. *Genizah?!* [A *Genizah* is a room in a synagogue in which old discarded manuscripts are stowed away. All the manuscripts of the synagogue are sacred and may not be destroyed. Sukenik assumed that the Dead Sea cave had been used for this purpose.]

"November 27, 1947: At X's [the dealer's] I saw four pieces of leather with Hebrew writing. The script seems ancient to me, very much like the writing on the Uzziah inscription. Is it possible? He says there are also jars. I looked a bit and found good Biblical Hebrew, a text unknown to me. He says a Bedouin of the Ta'amira tribe brought it to him.

"November 29, 1947: This morning I was at X's. Again I looked at the parchments, they suggest odd thoughts. In the afternoon I went with X to Bethlehem. I saw the jars, and it's difficult for me to say anything about their date. I took them.

"This evening we heard that the partition proposal had been accepted by more than a two-thirds majority. Congratulations!"

This was the partition of Palestine, which had been voted that day by the United Nations. The atmosphere was now very tense. Sukenik had consulted his son, an officer in Haganah, the underground Jewish defence group, as to whether the roads were safe enough for him to make the journey to Bethlehem. "As a military man," says the younger Sukenik (now General Yigael Yadin), "I answered that he ought not to make the journey; as an archaeologist, that he ought to go; as his son—that my opinion had to be reserved." The father had got through to Bethlehem and brought back all but one of the second lot of scrolls—which turned out to consist of three manuscripts (one of them in three pieces) and a handful of fragments. Open and savage hostilities broke out the next day. The Arabs tried to isolate the Jews by cutting off their communications with Tel-Aviv: they ambushed the

Jewish buses, burning them and shooting them up.

Sukenik's diary continues:

"December 1, 1947: X says that we shan't see one another in the near future because of the Arab strike, proclaimed for the next three days.

"I read a little more in the 'parchments.' I'm afraid of going too far in thinking about them. It may be that this is one of the greatest finds ever made in Palestine, a find we never so much as hoped for.

"December 5, 1947: More killings. The strike was over today, but not the violence. The find leaves me no peace. I'm bursting to know what will come of it all. It might turn out that the neighbourhood has many things of this sort. Who knows what surprises still await us?

"December 6, 1947: Night. I sit and think and think about the scrolls. When will I see more of them? Patience, patience.

"December 21, 1947: Days of awe. I contacted X. We're to meet tomorrow at noon near the gate [to the Security Zone].

"I came. I bought another scroll in very bad condition.

"January 13, 1948: I went to the main Post Office (near the border). X came. He promised to get in touch with Bethlehem. I said the *Hagomel* blessing as I left [a blessing to be said on occasions of escaping from mortal danger]."

"December 31, 1948: An historic year in our

people's history has concluded. A painful year—
Matti died, God bless him! [The author's youngest
son, lost in action as a fighter-pilot].

"Were it not for the *Genizah*, the year would have
been intolerable for me."

The excitement of discovering the scrolls had
enabled him partly to forget the war. At a time
when the Arab Legion had been shelling the offices
of the Jewish Agency in the middle of New Jerusalem, between three and five every afternoon, he had
not hesitated to call a press conference at this dan-
gerous place and hour, promising important news.
To attend it required some nerve. An American
correspondent fainted in the street on the way, and
had to be carried in by his colleagues. The reporters
were flabbergasted when Sukenik, who seemed quite
unperturbed by the flashing and banging about
him, announced the discovery of the Dead Sea
scrolls: except for a few scraps, as he told them, the
first ancient Hebrew manuscripts known. He thought
they must be as old as the first or second century B.C.
They heard the name of Isaiah, and something
about a hitherto unknown work to which Sukenik
had given the title, *The War of the Children of Light
against the Children of Darkness*. At the moment this
was mentioned, a shell burst. The reporters had at
first been rather peevish at having been asked to risk
their skins for old manuscripts, but they ended by
being impressed by the scholar's overmastering
enthusiasm.

It was, however, not till the February of 1948 that the Metropolitan Samuel succeeded in making contact with someone who could tell him about the scrolls. It was remembered by one of his monks, Brother Butros Sowmy, that he had been well received, ten years earlier, when he had had occasion to visit the American School of Oriental Research, and he suggested calling them up. This was done, and Brother Butros Sowmy took the scrolls there on February 18 and showed them to the then Acting Director, Dr. John C. Trever. The Director, Dr. Millar Burrows of the Yale Divinity School, was away on a trip to Iraq. Dr. Trever, a younger less experienced man, was not able at once to estimate, as Professor Sukenik had done, the probable age of the manuscripts, but when he began to suspect what they were, he, too, became much excited. "Remembering the box of slides in my desk," he writes in the *Biblical Archaeologist*, " on *What Lies Back of Our English Bible?*, I thumbed through them for the section on early Hebrew manuscripts. One glimpse at the picture of the British Museum Codex from the ninth century assured me that these scrolls were far older. The next slide was of the Nash Papyrus, a small fragment in the Manchester Library in England containing the *Shema* and the Ten Commandments." Now, the so-called Nash Papyrus, which was bought about fifty years ago from an Egyptian dealer by an Englishman, is written in an archaic script which at that time was otherwise hardly known, and it had usually been regarded as the oldest Hebrew manuscript in existence. It has been dated by various authorities from sometime early in the second pre-Christian century to sometime toward the end of the first century A.D. So it was natural that Dr. Trever should also have become exhilarated when he saw that "the similarity of the script in the papyrus and the scrolls was striking." But, he adds, "the picture was too small to help much." He had no camera there, so he copied out a passage from one of the scrolls and eventually identified it as a part of Isaiah. Later on, he persuaded the Metropolitan to allow him to photograph all the scrolls, convincing him that their value would be much increased if they were published and an interest in them stimulated. This decision, as we shall later see, was in some ways a very fortunate, and in other ways, a rather unfortunate one.

But nothing could be done at once. In the course of the battle for Jerusalem, the current had been cut off, and it was doubtful whether it would be possible to get light to photograph the manuscripts. While they were waiting—Dr. Trever and his colleague Dr. William H. Brownlee—they looked up, by kerosene lamps, everything they could find in the library that might throw light on the Nash Papyrus. By midnight they felt quite certain that the new Isaiah scroll was as old as, if not older than, this. "Sleep," writes Dr. Trever, "came with greater difficulty. The added evidence kept racing through my mind. It all seemed incredible. How could we be right?" The next morning the current came on; but there were fifty-four columns of Isaiah alone, and they were far from having got through them by noon, so the Syrians from the Monastery stayed to lunch. "The hour of fellowship around the table we shall long cherish," Trever writes, "for it gave us a feeling for ecumenical Christianity, and it brought us closer in our friendship and understanding of the Syrians." The Metropolitan, of course, was delighted that his faith in the antiquity of the scrolls had finally been justified. Not wanting to give away the cache to anyone who chose to go there, he had at first told the people at the school that the scrolls were uncatalogued manuscripts which had turned up in the monastery library; but later, when they had gained his confidence, he gave them the whole story. Dr. Trever, thereupon, explained to him that the antiquity laws of Palestine required that all such discoveries should immediately be reported, and the Metropolitan assured them that in future he would scrupulously co-operate with the Department of Antiquities and the school. After lunch, they returned to their task. Parts of the scrolls were in pieces, and they had to fit them together. They fastened them with Scotch Tape, but presently the tape gave out. They had been able to get through only two when the Syrians in the afternoon had to return to the monastery, but the Metropolitan left them two more, which turned out to be two sections of a single document. The smallest of the scrolls was so stuck together that they decided it constituted a problem which would have to be carefully considered, and the Metropolitan took it away.

Dr. Trever at once sent off prints of columns of the Isaiah scroll to Dr. W. F. Albright of Johns Hopkins, one of the greatest living Biblical archaeologists and an authority on the Nash Papyrus, which he had studied intensively over a period of years. They heard from him by air mail on March 15. He had written the same day he received the letter: "My heartiest congratulations on the greatest manuscript discovery of modern times! There is no doubt in my mind that the script is more archaic than that of the Nash Papyrus . . . I should prefer a date around 100 B.C. . . . What an absolutely incredible find! And there can happily not be the slightest doubt in the world about the genuineness of the manuscript."

In the meantime, Professor Sukenik had heard— but not till after he had bought the three manuscripts—from one of the University librarians who had been to the monastery, of the existence of the other five scrolls. Yet another Syrian merchant, having learned of Sukenik's interest, seems to have offered, without the Metropolitan's knowledge, to arrange to sell Sukenik the scrolls. Late in February, he came to the monastery and asked for permission to show them to Sukenik. The Metropolitan produced the photographs, but the go-between objected that these were too small. At a time when the fighting was fierce and the current again cut off, Sukenik met the Syrian merchant at night on the neutral ground of the Y.M.C.A., and with a flashlight examined the manuscripts. He persuaded the man to let him take them home, and kept them for two days, copying out several columns of Isaiah, which, to the owner's annoyance, he published. (There was a second Isaiah scroll—but in a very fragmentary state—among those that Sukenik had purchased.) He was eager to buy this other lot of manuscripts, and repeatedly sent emissaries to the monastery, but the Metropolitan Samuel had already signed an agreement with the Americans of the School, according to the terms of which he allowed them to publish the texts they had photographed, if they did so within three years. The Metropolitan, in return, was to receive fifty per cent of the profits from such publication.

The Americans at the School were eager to visit the cave, but the state of war made this impossible. The Mandate was to end at midnight of May 14, when it was plain that the Jews and the Arabs would finally be left to fight it out, and, for the scholars, the most pressing problem was to get out of the way in time. Before this had been arranged, the Metropolitan one day, without warning, sent a taxi, accompanied by a bodyguard, to bring Dr. Trever to the monastery. The American was apprehensive, but as soon as he arrived at St. Mark's, he was reassured to see its master standing at the top of the stairs and greeting him with a smile. "He took me into his office and handed me a folded sheet of paper. Within the fold was a piece of one of the scrolls! Instantly I recognized it as a portion of the scroll, for the colour of the leather on which it was written, the script, the size and the shape all coincided. The edges were eaten away by worms, as was the beginning of that scroll, and it looked exactly like the missing right-hand part of the first column, the absence of which had been such a disappointment to Dr. Brownlee when he was studying it. Half of a previous column was on it, also, proving that the scroll had originally had at least one more column at the beginning. . . . Needless to say, I lost little time in getting this new fragment photographed also." Dr. Trever was made even happier when "the Metropolitan informed me that Brother Butros had left that morning with all the manuscripts, to take them to a place of safety outside Palestine." This was what the Americans had recommended. They themselves got away a few days later.

The Mandate came to an end. The British simply departed. They had refused to allow their control to be transferred to any other body or to legalize a local militia. They were leaving the Jews and the Arabs already at one another's throats, and were counting on the seven Arab states arrayed against the small Jewish colony to fall upon it and destroy it or drive it out. The Arabs, under Brigadier Glubb, formerly of the British Army but now ranking as an officer of the Arab Legion, immediately began to shell the ancient Jewish quarter, which was isolated in the Old City. The monastery stood close to this and caught the fire from both sides. Brother Butros Sowmy was killed, and the monastery suffered damage which the Metropolitan estimated at £30,000. He did not, however, leave Jerusalem till the autumn, when the conflict had still not been settled. After sojourns in Transjordan and Syria, he sailed for the United States and arrived at the end of January, 1949, bringing the scrolls with him. Dr. Burrows, now back at Yale, had encouraged him to come to this country. The American School had arranged to publish the text of the scrolls, and the Metropolitan hoped that this would help him to sell the originals. But we must drop at this point his adventures with these, for here a new chapter begins.

# 2

# *The Essene Order*

PÈRE ROLAND DE VAUX of the Ecole Biblique and
Mr. G. Lankester Harding of the Department of
Antiquities, now Jordanian, not Transjordanian,
lost no time, when the war was over and the time of
year was favourable—February, 1949—in visiting
the cave where the scrolls had been found. They
worked there for nearly a month, and collected
many smaller fragments and a good deal of broken
pottery. This was thought to be mostly late Hellenis-
tic, but there were also some pieces of a Roman lamp
and a Roman cooking pot, and these latter gave rise
to a theory—for which there was no real evidence—
that they had been left in the cave by Origen, the
early Church Father and editor of the Biblical texts,
who fled from persecution to Palestine in the first
half of the third century and who says that he found
near Jericho some Biblical manuscripts in a jar. The

31

predominantly Greek pottery seemed to show that
the manuscripts could not have been written later
than the first Christian century. From the shards of
the jars they calculated that the cave must once have
contained a collection of at least two hundred scrolls.

When the word got around to the Bedouins that
the manuscripts from the caves were valuable, they
began to look in other caves, and in the latter part
of 1951 they turned up at the Ecole Biblique with
handfuls of crumbled papyrus and parchment that
were obviously the remnants of similar scrolls. De
Vaux at once called up Harding and told him that
they must move to take over the search. They descended on the Dead Sea (January 21, 1952), with
the Bethlehem Chief of Police and two soldiers from
the Arab Legion, and were guided by the Bedouins
to a group of four caves, about fifteen miles south of
the original cave, very high in the steep cliffs. Other
Bedouins, upon their arrival, came swarming out of
these holes like chipmunks. They sent a few to jail
with light sentences, and the Department of Antiquities hired the rest to carry on the search. Harding
and de Vaux now officially took over the exploration of all this region. There were four of these caves
—very large ones, about a hundred and fifty feet
long and fifteen feet high and wide. They had been
lived in at various periods. The earliest traces of
human habitation went back to the fourth millen-
nium before the Christian era. There were objects
from the Bronze Age and the Iron Age; and many

relics from the Roman period: a whole equipment for living—lamps, picks, javelin points, nails, needles, combs, buttons, spoons, bowls and plates made of wood, a chisel, a scythe and a trowel. There were also twenty Roman coins dating from Nero to Hadrian. Nine of these belonged to the years— 132-135 A.D.—of the Second Revolt of the Jews against the domination of the Romans. There were many fragments of manuscripts and potsherds that had been used for writing: Greek, Latin, Hebrew and Aramaic. There were several letters in Hebrew —one of them most amazing: a note written evidently in the midst of the war by the Jewish leader Bar-Kochba, in which he admonishes one of his captains. He speaks of "the Galileans," but without making it plain whom he means or what sort of role they are playing. (If these Galileans are Christians, we know that they had refused to support Bar-Kochba, in loyalty to Jesus, who had said, "My kingdom is not of this world.") Père de Vaux, from all this, has concluded that the cave was a stronghold of the Jewish resistance, and was eventually raided by the Romans. Two of the Roman coins are stamped with the galley of the Tenth Legion, and there are shreds of Torah scrolls, which look as if the Romans had torn them up.

Among the fragments of manuscript from these and other caves in the South, at least one important document has already come to light. We know that the Jews of the second century, at the time when

Christianity was having its first great success, became very much annoyed by the Christian exploita-
tion of the Septuagint for the purpose of showing, by
quotations from it, that the advent of Jesus as
Messiah had been predicted by the Prophets, and
that they, the Jews, had a version designed to dis-
credit this interpretation by bringing the Greek text,
as they claimed, closer to the meaning of the original
Hebrew. This problem is discussed at length in one
of the writings of Justin Martyr, the second-century
Christian convert and apologist—a dialogue which
is supposed to take place between Justin and the
Rabbi Trypho. Justin quotes several passages from
this Jewish translation and declares that, compared
to the Septuagint, they are obviously flat and inade-
quate. No such Jewish translation has hitherto been
known; but, by a great piece of luck for scholars,
some fragments of precisely these passages from the
Prophets that Justin cited to Trypho have turned
up among those found in these caves. This discovery
was made by Père D. Barthèlemy of the Ecole Biblique in Jerusalem, who has tracked down also in
other texts quotations from a Greek translation that
does not correspond with the Septuagint and that is
evidently from a Hebrew hand.

But these documents—though, of course, of great
interest—are not relevant to our main subject and
have apparently no connection with the discoveries
of Qumrân (as the Arabs called the wadi or ravine
near which the first scrolls were found). These were

now to be sensationally added to. The French monk and the English official had hardly finished with these other caves when new fragments of manuscripts were brought them from a cave near the first one explored. They set out now to examine systematically all the caves in the Qumrân neighbourhood. They entered two hundred and sixty-seven, and in thirty-seven of them found pottery and other relics of human occupancy. In twenty-five of these, the pottery was identical with the jars from the original cave. Several of the caves contained scrolls, which, unprotected by jars, were in a state of disintegration, often buried under layers of dirt. The fragments of these collected ran into tens of thousands. It was becoming more and more apparent that a library had been hidden here—a library which seems to have included almost all the books of the Bible, a number of apocryphal works and the literature of an early religious sect. The Essene sect had been thought of—for reasons I shall presently explain—as soon as the first scrolls were read. Mr. Harding and Père de Vaux had already, before finding these new manuscripts, had the notion of investigating a hitherto neglected old ruin not far from the original cave, and, in November and December of 1951, had started digging it out. This ruin was buried on the shore between the cliffs and the sea, a little to the south of the cave, with only a bit of stone wall showing above the ground. It has been known to the Arabs as the Khirbet Qumrân (*Khirbet* meaning *ruin*). A French traveller in 1851 believed it to be a remnant of the ruins of the Biblical Gomorrah. Later archaeologists have thought it a small Roman fort. It had never, up to that time, attracted very much attention; but it has been now almost completely excavated by Mr. Harding and Père de Vaux. What has been made to emerge is astounding: a very ancient stone building, containing from twenty to thirty rooms and thirteen cisterns for water, and with much of its equipment intact. On one side of it, between it and the sea, lies a cemetery with more than a thousand graves. The building has the look of a monastery, and a convergence of evidence seems not merely to suggest but almost beyond question to establish that it was one of the habitations, if not actually the headquarters, of what has previously been known as the Essene sect. But before we describe it further, we must explain who the Essenes were.

A good deal has already been known about this sect from three writers of the first century A.D.: Pliny, Josephus and Philo. Pliny's description is brief but very important in the present connection, for it locates the Essene community exactly where this building and the library were found. "On the western shore of the Dead Sea, the Essenes have withdrawn to a sufficient distance to avoid its noxious effects—a solitary people, and extraordinary beyond all others in the whole world, who live without women and have renounced all commerce with Venus, and also without money, having the palms for their only companions. They constantly renew themselves from the steady stream of refugees that resort to them in large numbers, men who, weary of life, have been driven by the vicissitudes of fortune to adopt their manner of living. Thus through thousands of centuries, incredible though it may seem, a people has perpetuated itself in which no one is ever born, so useful for recruiting their number is the disgust of other men with life. Below them the town of Engadda [Engedi] once stood— in its palm groves and general fertility second only to Jerusalem, but now a heap of ashes like it. Beyond this is Masada, a fortress on a rock, and itself not far from the Dead Sea. To this point Judea extends."

This seems definitely to identify the monastery; but it is all that Pliny tells us. He is summarily and tersely Roman; his point of view is alien and rather ironic. But Philo and Josephus, both Jews, have a good deal more interest in this Jewish order. The thousands of centuries with which Pliny credits it must either refer to the future or simply be due to his vagueness. It seems probable, from Josephus' account, that the Essenes had had their rise in the middle of the previous century. For Philo, the Alexandrian scholar, who had something himself of the monastic temperament, the Essenes supplied an example to illustrate the thesis of his *Treatise to Prove*

*that Every Good Man Is Also Free.* In this and in
another passage, quoted by the historian Eusebius,
he gives us accounts of the manners of the Essenes
that are appropriate to his purpose and congenial to
his own personality. But since Philo's accounts are
partly duplicated by the fuller account in Josephus,
it is easier to base one's description on this, noting
Philo's divergences from it and his amplifications of
Josephus' points. An historian and man of affairs,
Josephus portrays the Essenes somewhat more
realistically than Philo; and, since he was once a
member of the order himself, his account of it must
stand as authoritative. During his lifetime, Josephus
tells us, the three principal sects of the Jews have
been the Pharisees, the Sadducees and the Essenes.
He himself, by the age of nineteen, had, he says,
been through all three of them, and had also spent
three years in the desert, mortifying his flesh, with a
holy hermit named Bannus, who clothed himself
only with what grew on trees, ate only such food as
grew wild, and disciplined himself to chastity by
constant cold-water baths. From these various religious experiments, Josephus had emerged as a
Pharisee. He later took an active part in the wars of
the Jews with the Romans; but the struggle for
Jewish independence was already becoming des-
perate, and the drive toward asceticism, retreat
from the world, had evidently been strongly felt by
him. He deals with the Essenes at much greater
length than with either of the other sects.

The Essenes, says Josephus, are bound together
more closely than these other sects: they constitute,
in fact, a brotherhood which has something in common with the Pythagoreans. They have quite renounced pleasure, identifying it with vice, and school
themselves in temperance and self-control. "Marriage they disdain, but they adopt other men's
children, while yet pliable and docile, accepting
them as their kin and moulding them in accordance
with their own principles." (Philo differs from this:
he says that there are no youths or children among
them, that only the mature are admitted.) "They
do not, indeed," Josephus continues, "on principle,
condemn wedlock—the propagation thereby of the
race, but they wish to protect themselves against
women's wantonness, being persuaded that none of
the sex keeps her plighted troth to one man." This
is supplemented by Philo, who says that the Essenes
repudiate marriage, "because they clearly discern
it to be the sole or the principal danger to the
maintenance of the communal life, as well as because
they particularly practise continence. For no Essene
takes a wife, because a wife is a selfish creature,
excessively jealous and an adept at beguiling the
morals of her husband and seducing him by her
continued impostures. For by the fawning talk
which she practises and the other ways in which she
plays her part like an actress on the stage, she first
ensnares the sight and hearing, and then, when
these victims have, as it were, been duped, she

cajoles the sovereign mind. And if children come, filled with the spirit of arrogance and bold speaking, she gives utterance with more audacious hardihood to things which before she hinted covertly and under disguise, and casting off all shame she compels her husband to commit actions which are hostile to the life of fellowship. For he who is either fast bound in the love-lures of his wife, or under the stress of nature makes his children his first care, ceases to be the same to others and unconsciously has become a different man and has passed from freedom into slavery." The Essenes have renounced riches, also: they eat only the simplest fare, and they wear their clothes and their shoes to shreds before they will provide themselves with new ones.

Philo says that there are more than four thousand Essenes; Josephus that there are about four thousand (a large number for Palestine in those days). "They occupy no one city," says Josephus, "but settle in large numbers in every town." Philo, too, describes them as "dwelling in many towns of Judea," but says that they avoid the large cities and prefer to "live in villages". The great point that is made by both is that the Essenes have organized communities which are grouped around a centre, where they come together for meals and to which they are always responsible. They hold all their goods in common. New members must surrender their property to the order, and all must contribute to it their earnings. In return, they get everything they need. A steward or manager does all the buying and handles all the money. Keeping anything back is severely punished. Even the clothing is common property. They are supplied, says Philo, with thick cloaks for winter and light mantles for summer. There is no buying or selling among them, and anyone can take anything for nothing from his "brother"; but they cannot give presents to relatives except with the permission of their superiors. When they travel, they carry nothing along with them, except arms to defend themselves against bandits, for an Essene will be cordially received by any Essene community. There is, in fact, in every town where the Essenes have established a community, a member of the sect appointed to welcome arrivals from elsewhere and to see that they are taken care of. The sick are supported, if they cannot work; the old people are cared for, says Philo, even if they are childless, as if they had many children. Most of them, says Josephus, live to be over a hundred.

They cultivate the earth or devote themselves to peaceful arts (Philo). They are farmers, shepherds, cowherds, bee-keepers, artisans and craftsmen. They will not make instruments of war. They will not engage in commerce; they know nothing of navigation. There are among them no slaves and no masters. They maintain a fraternal equality, believing that human brotherhood is the natural relationship of men, which has only been destroyed in society by the competition of the covetous. They read much in the writings of the ancients, says Josephus (hence, no doubt, the many scrolls in the caves); yet (Philo) they do not cultivate the logical side of philosophy, do not expend "any superfluous care on examining Greek terms," but occupy themselves only with the moral side. They study medicinal roots and the properties of stones (these were probably charms); they are inspired in foretelling the future (several instances are given of this). They pay scrupulous attention to cleanliness and are always washing themselves. Their habits of defecation, for the Middle East of those days, were remarkably sanitary. They considered it defiling to rub oil on themselves—which must have exposed them painfully to the brutalities of the Mediterranean sun. They were compelled to keep a dry skin, and they always dressed in white. "In their costume and deportment," says Josephus, "they resemble children under rigorous discipline."

Their whole day is subjected to this discipline. They do not converse before the rising of the sun; they only recite traditional prayers, in which they entreat the sun to show himself. After this, they go out to their work, at which they continue till the fifth hour (about 11 o'clock). They pay no attention to weather, says Philo, and never use it as an excuse for not working; and they return from their work rejoicing, as if from an athletic contest. They then wash themselves with cold water, put on their linen raiment, and proceed to their refectory as if to a shrine. Here they sit down in silence, and are served by the baker with loaves, and by the cook with a plate of a single course. The presiding priest says grace and prays again at the end of the meal, after which they lay aside their linen clothes, treating them as holy vestments, and go back to their work in the fields or shops. At evening, they dine again, with any guests who may happen to be with them. No chatter or uproar: they speak in turn. "To persons from the outside," Josephus says, "the silence of those within gives the impression of some awful mystery." Silence for the Essenes is very important. When ten, a Jewish quorum, are sitting together, one of them will refrain from speaking if the other nine desire to be silent. They are stricter in observance of the Sabbath than any of the other sects; but they do not, like them, offer animal sacrifices: they do not believe in this practice, asserting they have purer lustrations of their own. The Essenes are, in consequence, excluded from the court of the Temple in Jerusalem, and apparently they never go near this centre of Jewish worship. In doctrine—whereas the Sadducees do not believe in immortality and think the soul dies with the body—the Essenes regard the body as corruptible but hold that the soul is imperishable. Emanating from the finest ether but dragged down by a natural spell, the spirit becomes caught in the prison of the body; but, once set at liberty by death, it rejoices and is born aloft. Like

43

the Greeks, the Essenes believe that the more virtuous souls have reserved for them, somewhere beyond the sea, a final place of retirement, where there is no snow or rain or heat, and which is always refreshed by a gentle breeze, while the baser ones will be committed to a murky and turbulent dungeon, where they will suffer eternal torment.

Josephus and Philo are agreed in emphasizing the general respect in which the Essenes are held. They surpass, the former declares, both the Greeks and the barbarians in virtue, and they have succeeded for many years in keeping up their high level of discipline. Both writers bring home to us the horror of the world from which the Essenes have withdrawn but which, morally, they have been able to stand up to. The Jews had had the Seleucid king Antiochus Epiphanes (inheritor of the Near Eastern section of the empire of Alexander the Great) setting up his statue of Zeus, "the abomination of desolation," to be worshipped by them in their Temple. They had successfully, under the Maccabees, revolted against the Seleucid tyranny—but only, before very long, to see their own rulers, among them the Herods, become as corrupt and as cruel as the foreigners they had displaced, and they had later, in 70 A.D., been defeated by the armies of the Roman Titus, who, like those of Nebuchadnezzar, had destroyed their temple. "Though at different times," says Philo, "a great number of potentates of every variety of disposition and character have occupied their country, some of whom have endeavoured to surpass even ferocious wild beasts in cruelty, leaving no sort of inhumanity unpractised, and have never ceased to murder their subjects in whole troops, and have even torn them to pieces while living, like cooks cutting them limb from limb—till they themselves, being overtaken by the vengeance of divine justice, have at last experienced the same miseries in their turn; others again, having converted their barbarous frenzy into another kind of wickedness, practising an ineffable degree of savagery, talking with the people quietly, but, through the hypocrisy of a more gentle voice, betraying the ferocity of their real disposition, fawning upon their victims like treacherous dogs, and becoming for them the causes of irremediable miseries, have left in all their cities monuments of their impiety and hatred of all mankind, in the never-to-be-forgotten sufferings endured by those they oppressed; and yet no one, not even of those immoderately cruel tyrants, nor of the more treacherous and hypocritical oppressors, was ever able to bring any real accusation against the multitude of those called Essenes or Holy Ones. But everyone, being subdued by the virtue of these men, looked up to them as free by nature, and not subject to the frown of any human being, and have celebrated their manner of messing together and their fellowship with one another—their mutual good faith is beyond description—which constitute sufficient proof of a perfect and supremely happy life."

45

Josephus, also, speaks of this fortitude and of the admiration it compels: "They make light of danger and triumph over pain by their resolute will; death, if it comes with honour, they consider better than immortality. The war with the Romans tried their souls through and through by every variety of test. Racked and twisted, broken and burnt, and made to pass through every instrument of torture, in order to induce them to blaspheme their Lawgiver or to eat some forbidden thing, they refused to yield to either demand, nor ever once did they cringe to their persecutors or ever shed a tear. Smiling in their agonies and mildly deriding their tormentors, they cheerfully resigned their souls, confident that they would receive them back again." Except for what Josephus calls the "terrible oaths" exacted from an initiate joining the order, they refuse to swear any oath, saying that "one who is not believed without an appeal to God stands condemned already"; and "any word of theirs," says Josephus, "had more force than an oath". He tells us that Herod the Great excused the members of the sect from taking an oath of loyalty; but makes it clear that this was due to the recollection that one of them, happening to see him in the street at a time when his political position was dubious, had "slapped him on the backside" and predicted that he would one day be king. This Essene had also predicted that Herod would later go bad; but the half-Jewish Herod, who was hated by the Jews, could afford, by the time he was reigning, to forget the unfavourable part of the prophecy and to show himself magnanimous by indulging the Essenes.

In reading these contemporary accounts of the Essenes, we are struck by two kinds of resemblances. For one thing, the modern traveller is often reminded of the Zionist and Israeli collective farms that are known as *kvutzot* and *kibbutzim*. Here the property is held in common, as that of the Essenes was; the purchasing is done by a manager or a management. The members of these communities have in some cases even shared their wardrobe, putting on any clothes that would fit them, as the Essenes did their winter and summer cloaks. Like the Essenes, they bring up adopted children—in the case of the Israeli communities, orphans and refugees. They have had to face tyrants as terrible as any that the Essenes fled from, and it has given them the same sort of impulse toward natural brotherhood that inspired the monasteries of the Essenes.

But the thing that we are immediately struck by is the resemblance of the Essenes to the Christians. You have the doctrine of human brotherhood; you have the practice of ritual washing, of which baptism was a prominent feature; you have communism, which the early Christians practised among themselves (Acts 2:44-45: "And all who believed were together, and had all things common;

and they sold their possessions and goods, and distributed them to all, as any had need"). You have phrases that bring Christian echoes. One finds Philo, for example, saying that the Essenes did not "store up treasures of silver and gold," nor "acquire vast sections of the earth out of a desire for ample revenues," and one remembers Matthew 6: "Lay not up for yourself treasures on earth," etc. When Josephus tells us that the Essenes held the body to be corruptible, but the soul immortal and imperishable, we think of I Corinthians 15:53: "For this corruptible must put on incorruption, and this mortal must put on immortality." You have the courage to defy the Romans, the "making light of danger" and the "triumph over pain". And—what is very important—you have the fact, which both Philo and Josephus make clear, that the Essenes, though of Jewish birth, have not come together on a basis of race, "for one does not speak of race when it is a question of voluntary acts". The Essenes have been brought together by their "zeal for virtue and by the passion of their love for mankind" (Philo). It seems obvious that the monastic tradition of the Christians must ultimately have derived from the Essenes, and there has always been a theory that Jesus was originally an Essene. This problem we must leave till later, when we discuss the unexpected revelations in connection with the origins of Christianity that have resulted from the Dead Sea scrolls. We should also remark, at this stage, that there were

elements in Essenism that sound as if they had come
from Persia or Babylonia: the non-Jewish rite of
baptism and the early-morning practice of sun-
worship.

Now, the manuscript pieced out by Trever from
two of the Metropolitan's scrolls turned out to be
the Manual of Discipline of an early monastic order,
and a comparison of this new document with the
descriptions of the Essenes quoted above has left
very little doubt as to what this order was. If the
passage from Pliny identifies the monastery, the
detailed account by Josephus identifies the Manual
of Discipline, which was found in the cave near the
monastery. Josephus must have studied this hand-
book, or one very much like it. His summary of
Essene procedure tallies almost exactly with the
Manual. We learn from both these documents, for
example, that the Essene principle of human
brotherhood was combined with a stringent hierarchy. The candidate, Josephus tell us, is not admitted the first year. He is given his white clothing,
his loincloth and a small mattock for digging his
own latrines. "He is brought into closer touch with
the rule and is allowed to share the purer kind of
holy water, but is not yet received into the meetings
of the community." He has then to be tested for two
years more, and if he qualifies at the end of that
period, he is allowed to share the common food, but
he must first swear "terrible oaths—first that he will
practise piety toward the Deity, next that he will

D                    49

observe justice toward men: that he will wrong none, whether of his own mind or under another's orders; that he will forever hate the unjust and fight the battle of the just; that he will forever keep faith with all men, especially with the powers that be, since no ruler attains his office save by the will of God; that, should he himself bear rule, he will never abuse his authority, nor, by his dress or by any other external mark of superiority, allow himself to outshine his subjects; to be forever a lover of truth and to expose liars; to keep his hands from stealing and his soul pure from unholy gain; to conceal nothing from the members of the sect and to report none of their secrets to others, even though tortured to death. He swears, moreover, to transmit their rules exactly as he himself received them; to abstain from robbery; and in like manner carefully to preserve the books of the sect and the names of the angels. Such are the oaths by which they secure their proselytes." The humility imposed on the Essene, the commitment not to "abuse his authority" or to display "outward marks of superiority" may remind us of the "Let not yourselves be called masters, for Christ is your only master" of Matthew 23:10. Yet with the Essenes the grades of seniority were maintained in the strictest fashion at the community meals and elsewhere. "So far," says Josephus, "are the junior members inferior to the senior that a senior, if but touched by a junior, must take a bath, as if after contact with an alien."

The injunction to keep faith with the powers that be may remind us of the "Render therefore unto Caesar the things that are Caesar's; and unto God the things that are God's" of Matthew 22:21. So inevitably does it seem to be true that definitive political defeat, the disappointment of practical hopes, gives rise to an intensive development of the more unworldly kind of religion. An obvious recent example is the efflorescence of mysticism in Russia after the failure of the Revolution of 1905. We are today going through something similar, at a time when disillusion with socialism, following close on a loss of confidence in the traditional competitive system, has been driving the bewildered idealists to look for comfort in the various churches. Now, the Jews, in the days of the Essenes, had succeeded in reviving their state under the leadership of the Maccabees, but had later taken a terrible beating at the hands of the more organized and "modern" Romans. The Essenes, who, though they possessed certain doctrines and followed certain practices of their own, were still basically Judiastic, had to assume, like the Old Testament prophets, that their miseries had been willed by God. The Jesus of the Christian Gospels seems to belong to a later stage, when God has been dissociated from Caesar; but once this break has been made, the Christian is in some ways in a stronger position than the priests who drew up the Essene oath. The Essenes are smarting and sullen—we find their attitude toward their enemies stated bitterly and in most un-Christian terms in the Manual and other writings; the Gospels have a heartening ring of audacity and spiritual freedom. Yet it was also, as it now appears, the sectarians that had framed this oath who were preparing, by their precept and discipline—"to report none of their secrets, even though tortured to death"—the resounding moral triumph of the Crucifixion.

Our main interest at this point, however, is to check the Manual of Discipline with the accounts of Josephus and Philo. You find here the property held in common and entrusted to a "custodian of property" (the phrase is that of the Manual); the devotion to the Lawgiver (presumably Moses), qualified by the substitution of "a fragrant offering of righteousness and perfection" for the traditional animal sacrifice; the lustrations in holy water; the insistence on self-control: one is fined for giving way to anger; the subordination, within the order, of "the lesser" to "the greater, in regard to goods and means"; the common table and the sacred repasts; the speaking in turn; the prerogatives of the majority, who can even keep someone from talking if the sentiment of the company is against it; the prohibition—also mentioned by Josephus—against "spitting into the midst of the session of the many." You have the probationary period—of a year, says Josephus; the Manual does not specify exactly—at the end of which the neophyte is permitted (similar phrases are used) to "draw close" to the order; then two more years of novitiate, in the course of which he is allowed to share in the "purification" (Manual), "purer kind of holy water" (Josephus), but not yet admitted to the meetings; if he successfully completes this novitiate, he swears the "terrible oaths" and thereafter partakes of the common meals. You find, also, in the Manual of Discipline, a good many other details that are not in Josephus or Philo. There is the whole code of censure and punishment, by which the discipline of the sect was enforced, that is omitted from Philo's idyllic picture. This system is rigorous and drastic enough, but Josephus explains that the Essenes were "just and scrupulously careful in their trial of cases, never passing sentence in a court of less than a hundred members." But the decision, once reached, is irrevocable. Those who are expelled from the order find themselves in a difficult situation, for the oaths they have taken forbid them any food not prepared by the order, and they may try to live on grass and "waste away." But the order will then sometimes take pity on them, believing they have been punished enough, and has actually received a good many back. "One shall not speak to his brother," says the Manual, "in anger or in complaint . . .; nor shall he hate him [in the uncircumcision] of his heart—though he shall reprove him on the very day so as not to incur guilt because of him. Indeed, a man shall not bring accusation against his fellow in the presence of the many who has not been subject to [previous] reproof before witnesses." Professor Brownlee, in a note to his translation of the Manual, points out that Matthew 18:15-17 "gives us the clue for interpreting the passage. Jesus specifies three stages for dealing with an erring brother: (1) personal reproof; (2) reproof before witnesses; (3) reproof before the Church."

One very important aspect of the teaching of the sect is indicated by Josephus only, without special emphasis, when he is summarizing the oath: the new member is made to swear "that he will forever hate the unjust and fight the battle of the just." In the Manual we find this theme elaborated at length in a section which describes the division of all mankind into two antithetical groups, dominated, respectively, by a Spirit of Darkness and a Spirit of Light. The Children of Darkness are angrily denounced. Though it was wrong to hate a brother in the faith, or even to lose one's temper, it was a duty to loathe and to curse the alien and wicked people which was dominated by the Spirit of Darkness. We shall later, when we come to the other scrolls, return to this feature of the literature of the sect. It is enough for the present to say that the Children of Darkness were probably the Romans, at the hands of whom the Jews had suffered so much.

# 3

## The Monastery

THE LANDSCAPE of the Dead Sea wilderness is
monotonous, subduing and dreadful. This country
is completely impersonal. It is a landscape without
physiognomy: no faces of gods or men, no bodies
of recumbent animals, are suggested by the shapes
of the hills. "Nothing but monotheism could
possibly come out of this," said one of my companions, who knew Palestine well. "There's no crevice
for a nymph anywhere." The already fading grass
of spring—my visit was in early April—had the
look of greenish mould on enormous loaves.
Tawny without warmth, of a dun not enriched by
shadow, these mounds also somewhat resembled—
it was the only living image one could think of—
the humps of the camels that grazed them, dull
yellow and gawkily bending, with their dusty
white calves beside them. One hillside was flecked

55

by a herd of black goats. Here and there, all alone in the emptiness, squats motionless a Bedouin woman, who, though she seems as unperceptive as a boulder, is keeping an eye on a camel or goat; and we pass a few torn and black Bedouin shelters that might be the old tents of Abraham. A watch-tower, now deserted, is still standing at a spot where, before the war, a plant run by Jews made potash, and there are ruins of a little inn that was fought over by the Jews and Arabs, who damaged it severely, and finally plundered by Bedouins. As the road begins to drop below sea-level—at the bottom, almost thirteen hundred feet—you feel pressure increasing on your ear-drums, as you do coming down in a plane.

Arriving at the Sea itself, you find two or three simple buildings, where a British officer of the Arab Legion presides over the "Dead Sea Fleet". This consists of a few small motor-boats that are kept here to patrol the frontier, since Israel begins just south of here, not far from where Pliny said Judea stopped. He has two little mongrel dogs, and he is able to invite us to tea. The Dead Sea is a dull pale blue that reminds one of the Great Salt Lake, and the hills across the water that wall it in are of yellows and purples and blues and browns so dull that such words for colour are almost too vivid to refer to them. One of them is Mount Nebo, from which Moses, when he had rescued his people from Egypt and wandered for years in the wilderness, looked across at the Promised Land.

We jolt in our jeep over backbreaking rocks, where the track of an ancient road has lately been just made out. The all but bare ground is rusted with streaks of some reddish plant, and dabbed here and there with statice, a dreary little white everlasting. The palms that were noted by Pliny as the only companions of the Essenes must have disappeared centuries ago. The only forms of vertebrate life that we see as we drive toward the monastery are a hawk and a crow contending for some small animal that the crow has caught but the hawk has forced him to drop. The crow is reluctant to leave his prey, but the hawk keeps on circling, incisively and slowly, and the crow has to keep a sharp watch on him. There are scorpions and vipers here, several of the latter of which the excavators have had to kill. It recalls that "great and terrible wilderness" of which Moses speaks in Deuteronomy 8:15, with its "fiery serpents and scorpions and thirsty ground, where there was no water". There are no fish in the heavy sea, but only microscopic animalcula. The landscape has something, perhaps, of Greece, yet there is nothing of the exquisite spectrum of violet, mauve and blue that is a function of the fluid Greek light. One is aware of neither light nor darkness. It is as if one were sunk below them; to live here seems a sort of self-burial. The visitor from the modern world, confronted by the blank of this region, is forced to

make an effort of imagination to convince himself
that anything interesting can ever have happened
in it. Yet one finds oneself here in the "wilderness"
where the word of God came to John the Baptist;
and, not far to the north, at the point where the
Jordan flows into the Dead Sea, is the place to which
Jesus came to be baptized by John. This arid depres-
sion in the earth is also that wilderness where Jesus
is supposed to have fasted for forty days. On our
way here, we have passed the mountain upon which,
according to tradition, Jesus was tempted by Satan,
who showed him from it the kingdoms of the world.
On the equally desolate opposite shore, Herod the
Great built Machaerus, the formidable stronghold
described by Josephus, where John the Baptist was
imprisoned and beheaded by the younger Herod.
This fortress was built on a very high rock with
deep ravines on all sides, and enclosed by a great
wall that had hundred-foot towers at the corners.
Near it were many springs, some bitter and some
sweet, of a variety of temperatures, including two
that flowed from two rocks like breasts, one hot
and the other cold; and inside the magnificent
palace, there is said to have grown an enormous
plant that was the colour of flame by day and at
twilight was seen to shine—a plant which eluded
the grasp of persons who tried to pluck it and
poisoned them if they succeeded, which could only
be paralyzed by pouring on it the urine or the
menstrual fluid of a woman. This plant had the

valuable property of expelling the devils from people possessed; but the only safe way to get hold of it was to first have it pulled up by the roots. The way to do this was to dig away the earth and tie a dog to these roots; the dog's master would then go away, and the dog would run after him and jerk up the plant. As a result of this operation, the dog would at once fall dead, but it would now become possible to handle the plant. When Judea fell finally to Titus, Machaerus was the last fortress taken: the Romans caught a spirited youth called Eleazar and scourged him in sight of the citadel, then erected a cross in plain view and threatened to crucify him. This forced the Jews to surrender, and the garrison, as promised, were allowed to go free; but the Romans made a point of murdering the seventeen hundred men in the town at the foot of the cliff, and enslaved their women and children. And across the lake from Machaerus, to the place to which our jeep has now brought us, the Essenes once resorted to worship God and to save their souls from these infamies; to turn away from the Way of Darkness and follow the Way of Light.

Their monastery, build crudely of grey blocks of stone, still stands, as was noted by Pliny, some distance away from the shore. The cliff rises steep behind it, and one catches sight, here and there, of the dark cracks of natural caves such as the one in which the scrolls were found. Between the Dead Sea and the monastery spreads the cemetery of a thousand graves. Père de Vaux has opened nineteen of these, and they are all more or less the same. The skeletons lie on their backs, with their heads in the direction of the south, and their hands crossed on the pelvis or stretched straight along the sides. What is singular about these graves is that there is almost nothing in them but bones. Only one of those opened contained a coffin. It is unusual to find ancient graves without some sort of funeral objects: ornaments or weapons or receptacles for food, signs of rank or distinction or equipment for the journey to the other world. The absence of such objects in these graves would seem to be perfectly appropriate to the reported austerity of the Essenes, but it makes them rather uninteresting to excavate. There have, however, been found in them, among the fragments of jars that seem to have got there accidentally, a few that belong to a type which has not hitherto been known except for a single specimen. This specimen, dug up from the citadel of Jerusalem, has been dated in the first B.C. century, before the constructions of Herod the Great. Père de Vaux has now ceased to explore the graves, but he has pretty well established one important point. The bones are very fragile and were sometimes found crushed, but a careful examination shows that one of the skeletons is certainly a woman's, and that two or three others may be. To have women connected with the order at all was, in general, as we have seen, contrary to the practice of the Essenes; but

Josephus—in a postscript to his main account—
explains that one branch of the sect does allow its
members to marry: "They think that those who
decline to marry cut off their chief function of life,
the propagation of the race, and, what is more,
that, were all to adopt the same view, the whole
race would very quickly die out. They give their
wives, however, a three years' probation." Pliny,
it will be remembered, says specifically of this community that they did not admit women; but, in this
case, his information may have been out of date or
inaccurate.

Before going on to the monastery itself, I must
give some account of Père Roland de Vaux, who
does not in the least resemble any of the conventional conceptions of a typical French priest. It may
be that the French character is today to be seen at
its best, not in the literary men, the politicians and
the antiquated generals about whom we mostly
hear, but in persons who have been lucky enough
not to share in the decay of France, who have had
some overmastering interest that kept them out of
the country or sustained them through the years of
demoralization. One felt, in reading *The Silent World*,
by the deep-sea diver Cousteau that here, rather
unexpectedly, was to be seen something of true
French greatness: good sense combined with daring,
the capacity under all conditions—in this case, the
resistance to inhuman pressures, breathing from a
tank at the bottom of the sea—for realistic and

accurate observation, for exercising a cool intelli-
gence. Such figures, it seems to me, are more satisfactory than most of the people one reads about in,
say, André Gide's journal, or even than Gide himself. I had of Père de Vaux, in his different department, an impression somewhat similar: intellect,
expertness, fortitude, tenacity, an element of daring
and—what now seems so rare in France—effective-
ness. He has brown eyes of the high-powered
headlight kind that seem magnified by his glasses'
thick lenses, and long white regular teeth that are
always displayed in talking. His sharp nose is of a
salience and aquilinity that strongly suggest the
Old Testament, as does his coarse bristling brown
beard. With his belted white-flannel Dominican
robe, the hood of which falls back on his shoulders
and at the belt of which hang his beads, he wears a
beret, heavy shoes and what look like substantial
blue golf stockings. He tells stories extremely well,
continually smokes cigarettes and altogether has
style, even dash. In the archaeological world, there
persists a curious legend that, before becoming a
Dominican, Père de Vaux was an actor in the
Comédie Française. This is, I think, a gratuitous
inference, drawn from his eloquence as a speaker
and from something that suggests a stage presence,
by the scholars of the American School, who do not
perhaps appreciate how much time and work it
takes to qualify as an actor at the Comédie. The
story has, in any case, been denied, with amaze-

ment, by de Vaux himself, who explains that his
education has been "wholly classical and clerical".
I did not find him theatrical: he seemed to me quite
unselfconscious, and intent on his work with a gusto
that almost amounted to voracity. I was struck by his
vigour one day when I happened to see him striding
out of the Tenebrae service at the Church of the
Holy Sepulchre, quickly outdistancing the rest of
the crowd—in what I suppose was a dark robe of
ceremony, his face burnt a brown brick-red, his
boarlike nostrils and beard pressing on to their next
destination. On the site of his excavations, among
the ruins and rocks, he climbs on short legs like a
goat. He evidently loves the rough side of it;
discards his clerical costume and puts on working
clothes. He has camped out on the "dig" for days.
Once they shot a hyena, he tells us. They ate it:
it was "very good," something like wild boar.
They hung it a long time, then boiled it, spicing it
well. I could imagine him proceeding intrepidly
along the almost razorback top of a narrow and
wall-like formation, in a cave in the prow of which
one of the biggest caches of scrolls was found. This
cave had been spotted by a Bedouin when a part-
ridge he had been hunting flew into it. It is situated
high in the rock, and at first they had used ropes
to climb into it; but they later made a hole in the
top of the ridge and thus opened another entrance,
which had to be approached along this ridge. It
looked almost like tight-rope walking, but Père de

Vaux said that it had not taken him long to come to feel as much at ease with it as if it had been merely a question of going up and down stairs in his own house.

He was delighted to take people there, but the very idea made me giddy. It even made me giddy to climb with him to the top of the monastery's highest wall—fifteen feet above the ground—and to perch there, clinging to the stones, while Père de Vaux expounded the building to us. He was giving us a bird's-eye view. The main structure presents a large rectangle, ninety-eight by a hundred and twenty feet, made of rudely cut blocks of stone joined with earthen mortar. There are windows, and the walls inside are plastered. The floor has been paved with pebbles. Layers of ashes seem to show that the roofing, probably made out of the Dead Sea reeds, had eventually been burned, and the empty mould left by the trunk of a palm suggests that it was used as a beam or for some kind of central support. In the northwestern angle stood a two-story tower, evidently used for defence, the basement of which was a storehouse. Inside the monastery proper, there are a kitchen, which has been identified by the oven and the hole in the wall for a flue; and what was presumably the refectory of the sacred repasts, close to which were found neatly stacked about a thousand jars and bowls. Another chamber, seventy-two feet long, has the look of an assembly room, with a platform of stone at one end that may perhaps have served as a pulpit from which the sacred books were read. A room with tables and benches constructed of plaster and brick was evidently a *scriptorium*, where the scrolls were copied out. Three inkwells were also found here—one of bronze, which has turned green, and two of terra cotta, turned black—in which there is still some dried ink. The brotherhood presumably made their pens from the reeds that grew by the lake-shore. There is a pottery, with a kind of round nest of stones, which may have held the potter's wheel; and a mill for grinding grain, of which the two parts, for some reason not known, turned up in different rooms. Lying about in various places were nails, locks and keys, hoes, scythes and pruning knives. There was a jar which resembles exactly the jars in which the first lot of scrolls were preserved, as both resemble the fragments found in 1952 in the newly discovered caverns; and there are lamps which match those in the caves.

Among the most striking features of the monastery are the six large cisterns, with steps leading down into them, upon which the inmates depended for water. Into these cisterns they evidently canalized the rains that descended by a trough from the hills and of which the supply was undoubtedly scant. Père de Vaux says that only twice in all the months of the three years he has worked here has he seen any water come down from these hills. The Essenes must have had to store, in the relatively rainy season, all their water for the rest of the year. And they had, also on the surface level, seven smaller cisterns—of which some of the piping can still be seen—which must have been used for "lustrations" and the baptisms of which so much is said in the literature of the sect (seven, for the Jews, was a mystical number). There are even two little cupped hollows in the room where the scrolls were copied, which must have been basins for washing in connection with this holy work. Another basin is probably a cesspool. Unaccountably, one finds here and there the traces of some more pretentious building: square stones and sections of column that must once have been the parts of a portico or colonnade, and two queerly placed bases of columns set. close together in the ground, as if they had been stands for something. Scattered about the building were about four hundred coins. No coins have been found in the Qumrân caves; and this perfectly fits in with what we are told by Philo and Josephus: that the finances of the Essene brotherhood were entirely handled by a manager. De Vaux has concluded that the members of the community lived in the nearby caves, and also in huts or tents—since pottery and large forked poles have been found stuck away in crevices or sheltered by overhanging rocks in a way which would seem to indicate that they had been concealed or stored by people who were living outside the caves. The building would have been their centre, to which they would have been fully

66

admitted only after they had completed their probation.

To trace the conclusions to which Père de Vaux has been led by the evidence supplied by this site and by the known facts of history enables one to feel some of the beauty and experience some of the excitement of the methods of modern archaeology, which have developed now so far past the stage when the excavator plundered the "dig" for objects of conspicuous interest, leaving the various layers— which might represent whole cities, whole periods— in chaos. The procedures in use at present aim at something like scientific accuracy, and record every stratum successively before digging on to the next. From the pottery, the coins and the stonework, and from various other indications, Père de Vaux and the men working with him have arrived at the following chronology of the history of the Qumrân building. There have been found, first of all, some remnants of a very ancient Israelite wall, which de Vaux dates about 700 B.C., and which he believes to have had no connection with the later developments of the site. The later construction, he thinks, was begun in the late second century B.C. The first close sequence of coins commences with Antiochus VII in 136 B.C. and runs through the Hasmonean period to 37 B.C.—that is, it covers the period of Jewish independence and extends to the accession of Herod the Great. The next group begins with the reign of his son, Herod Archaelaus (4 B.C.-6 A.D.), and extends to 68 A.D. There would seem to have been an interval, then, when the building was left unoccupied. (Two coins from this interval between the two sequences may be easily accounted for by their happening to have been still in circulation when the building was eventually reoccupied.) Another big gap occurs between 68 and 132 A.D., but there are thirteen coins that belong to the period of Bar-Kochba's final revolt against the Romans in 132-135, and all of these later coins were found on the same level of soil.

In view of the fact that there are many coins from the reigns of the late Jewish kings, John Hyrcanus and Alexander Jannaeus, Père de Vaux thinks it probable that the monastery was built in the reign of the former (136-106 B.C.) and occupied during that of the latter (104-78 B.C.). The whole period of the occupancy of the Essenes would have extended from the end of the second century B.C. up to the year 68 A.D. But how to explain the hiatus between 37 and 4 B.C.? Certain signs seem to show that the monastery was damaged at some point by an earthquake. There is a fissure that runs all through the steps to one of the big cisterns and which can be traced in the rest of the building; the tower has been reinforced with stones that are banked about the base; and there is a room with a propped-up wall that seems to have been closed and condemned. Now, the date of this upheaval would seem to be determined, again by the invaluable

Josephus, who tells us that in the seventh year of the reign of Herod the Great, not long before the Battle of Actium—which would put it in the spring of 31—Judea was shaken by an earthquake, in which thirty thousand people were killed. The building would not have been reoccupied—as the coins of Archelaus show—till somewhere near the beginning of the Christian era. But why did the community wait thirty years before moving back into the monastery? Père de Vaux has suggested that there is documentary evidence which may throw some light on this problem, and this I shall explain in a moment, when we arrive at the document in question. It may be noted, in the meantime, that loads of debris, apparently left by the earthquake, were removed from the building and piled outside, where they are still to be recognized.

But the Romans in the end got the Essenes—either killed them or caused them to flee. In the second year of the first Jewish revolt—67-68 A.D., when the second sequence of coins ends—the building must have been destroyed. There are broken-down walls, signs of burning and iron arrow-heads lying about. After the Roman operations of 67—we return to Josephus' narrative—the Tenth Legion was encamped at Caesarea on the Mediterranean, and in June of the following year, Vespasian paid a visit to Jericho and the Dead Sea. He was curious to find out for himself whether the latter was as heavy as people said, and he had some of his men who could not swim thrown into the water with their hands tied behind them. He noted that they rose to the surface. A few of the monastery coins seem to belong to this Roman visit, since one of them is stamped with an X, which would indicate the Tenth Legion. The legionaires must have remained there at least well into the reign of Titus—sometime after 79 A.D.—as is shown by three coins stamped *Judæa Capta*. This Roman post is explained by the special facilities of the monastery site for keeping a watch on the shore from the mouth of the Jordan to Râs Feshkha, and overlooking the whole northern half of the sea. The Romans had also to deal with the fortress of Masada, not far south of the monastery. This had been captured in 66 by the Jews, who had slaughtered the Roman garrison and who succeeded in holding it till April of 73, three years after the fall of Jerusalem. There was only one point that was vulnerable, and this the Romans finally breached with a battering ram, but then found themselves confronted with a bulwark, which the occupants had just put up; this the besiegers eventually burned. Inside, they found alive only two women and five children. All the rest of this stubborn remnant of nine hundred and sixty Jews had been induced by their leader to kill themselves. He had reminded them, according to Josephus, that they had "long ago resolved never to be servants to the Romans, nor to any other than God Himself."

That the ruin was used again during the second Jewish revolt is indicated by the coins from that period. Ten of these coins were found in the dugout at the bottom of the tower. Whoever now occupied the building had shut off the whole southeastern end of it. "The building has changed its function," says de Vaux. "It no longer shelters the general services of an organized community. It serves only as habitation for a limited group of persons, who lodge in the little rooms, cook their bread in the oven . . . protect themselves from attacks . . . and keep a lookout in the tower." When the Romans had subdued this second revolt, the building was abandoned forever. Two Arab and three Byzantine coins that were found at the surface level must have been left by travellers who camped there. We do not know what became of the Essenes.

# 4

## The Teacher of Righteousness

WE DO NOT know what became of the Essenes; but
we do know a good deal more now—since the
discovery of the Dead Sea library—about what had
been happening to them, how they lived and what
they believed. It ought to be said at this point that
the evidence of the ancient coins—which seems to
show that the occupancy of the sect, preceded no
doubt by their presence in the region, must have
extended from about the last third of the second
pre-Christian century (with a thirty-year interrup-
tion) at least to 68 A.D., the eve of the victory of
the Romans—appears definitely to settle, in a general way, the dating of the manuscripts, about
which, before the excavation of the ruin, there had
been much rather violent controversy. We can form
no idea, of course, except from internal evidence,
as to when the works copied were written, but it

seems clear that the copies could not have been made any later than the descent of the Romans, at which moment the manuscripts were hidden in caves—like the one which de Vaux risked his neck to reach—that were as hard to get at as possible. This fits in with the date assigned by Albright who, arguing from the palaeographical evidence, immediately put the Isaiah scroll at about 100 B.C.; with the conclusions of the pottery experts, who said that the jars were pre-Herodian and dated them not later than the end of the last century B.C.; and with radio-carbon tests, which, applied to the linen wrappings, gave a range of possibility between 168 B.C. and 233 A.D.

Not only did the documents found combine with the passages in ancient writers and the discovery of the monastery itself to make it possible to form some conception of a remarkable religious movement of which little hitherto had been known; but, in relation to certain other late Hebrew writings, known but not fully understood, which had already been assigned to this same general period, the new manuscripts at once set up what may be likened both to a chain reaction and to the clustering of iron filings around a magnet.

First of all, there were the so-called Zadokite fragments. These are parts of a document or documents that were discovered at Cairo in 1896, in excavating the *Genizah* of a medieval synagogue. The manuscripts are supposed to date from sometime

between the tenth and the twelfth centuries A.D.;
but the original writings themselves must derive
from the same source, and hence date from the
same period, as those of the Dead Sea monastery.
This seemed obvious from the first lot of scrolls,
since the Zadokite document expounds the same
doctrines, deals with the same events, and even
makes use of the same language, as the Manual of
Discipline and others of the scrolls; but the matter
has now been put beyond doubt by the findings in
one of the other caves of several fragments of the
"Zadokite" text. I shall not, therefore, list the close
resemblances between these and the other documents; I shall simply count them in with the others
when I come to describe, in a moment, the history
and doctrine contained in this whole body of writing.
Two points should, however, be mentioned. Neither
these fragments nor the Manual of Discipline nor
any other of the writings yet found ever refers to the
members of the sect as Essenes. In the Manual, as in
the fragments, its priests are always the "sons of
Zadok"; and its laity is not given any special name.
Now, we do not know for certain who this Zadok
was. It is believed, however, by nearly all scholars
that the Zadok of the Bible is meant: the priest who
anointed Solomon—since it is said, in one of the
fragments, in connection with the polygamy of
David, that when David had forgotten the Law, it
was rediscovered by Zadok. The Essenes, as
appears from the ancient descriptions, regarded

themselves as reformers, and these fragments describe a conflict with the official priests of Jerusalem which resulted—the second fact to note—in a migration of the sect to Damascus. This migration, Père de Vaux suggests, may account for the abandonment of the monastery over the unexplained period of thirty years. The discrepancy between the name that was given the dissident group by the authors who have written about it and the name that they gave themselves has been accounted for by the theory that the order were called Essenes, "Holy Ones," only by outsiders. In future, I shall follow the example of other writers on the subject in referring to them simply as "the sect," "the brotherhood" or "the order."

But, besides the so-called Zadokite work (sometimes known as the Damascus document), there are at least four apocryphal Old Testament books that evidently have close connections with the literature of the sect: *The Book of Jubilees, The Book of Enoch, The Testaments of the Twelve Patriarchs* and *The Assumption of Moses.* These works have been dated somewhat differently by two of the leading scholars in this field of Old Testament apocrypha—R. H. Charles and C. C. Torrey—but the divergences are not very great, and Charles and Torrey are agreed that these writings were produced, in their present form—chronologically in the order named—between the second half of the second century B.C. and the early years of the first century A.D. Though

they had hitherto been known only in translation—
Greek, Latin or Ethiopic—it had already been
assumed that the originals were in Hebrew or
Aramaic. This assumption and the dating are now
confirmed by the tie-up with the Dead Sea scrolls.
Aside from the internal evidence of subject and
phraseology, we have a reference to *The Book of
Jubilees* in a passage of the Zadokite fragments, in
connection with the novel calendar which the
dissident sect adopted and which cut them off—
since their holy days now came on different dates—
from orthodox Jewish worship; and a fragment of
*Jubilees* itself as well as fragments of *Enoch* and
*The Testaments of the Twelve Patriarchs*, in what are
evidently the original Hebrew and Aramaic texts,
have turned up among the Qumrân writings.

A tie-up with the literature of the Christians is
shown by the direct quotation in the New Testament Epistle of Jude (14) of a passage from *The
Book of Enoch*; by an obvious reference in Jude 9 to
an episode in *The Assumption of Moses*—the struggle,
over the body of Moses, of the Archangel Michael
with Satan; and by passages in the *Twelve Patriarchs*,
to which we shall come in a moment. And there are
also unmistakable resemblances between all these
pre-Christian or non-Christian writings and certain
works that were once accepted as part of the Christian canon but later rejected from it.

An extra dramatic touch was given the whole
situation when Professor Otto Eissfeldt of Halle

called the attention of scholars to a document—
first published in 1901—that must date from somewhere near the beginning of the ninth Christian
century. This was a letter from a Patriarch of
Seleucia to a Metropolitan of Elam. "We have
learned," the Patriarch writes, "from trustworthy
Jews who were then being instructed as cate-
chumens in the Christian religion, that some books
were found ten years ago in a rock-dwelling near
Jericho. The story was that the dog of an Arab out
hunting went into a cave in pursuit of game and
did not come out again; its owner went in after it
and found a chamber in the rock, in which there
were many books. The hunter went off to Jerusalem
and told his story to the Jews, who came out in
great numbers and found books of the Old Testament and others in the Hebrew script; and, since
there was a scholar well read in literature among
them, I asked him about many passages which are
quoted in our New Testament [as] from the Old
Testament but are not found anywhere in it, either
in copies in the hands of the Jews or in those in the
hands of the Christians. He said [that] they are
there and can be found in the books discovered
there. When I heard this from the catechumen and
had also interrogated the other without his being
present, and heard the same story without variations,
I wrote about it" to friends in that part of the world
and asked them to look up these manuscripts and
check "whether the passage 'He shall be called a

Nazarene' [Matthew 2:23], and other passages quoted in the New Testament as from the Old Testament but not found in the text which we have, could be discovered anywhere in the Prophets." He asked also about the passage: "Have pity upon me, O God, according to Thy mercy . . . sprinkle me with the hyssop of the blood of Thy cross and cleanse me" (which does not occur in our New Testament, but is evidently a Christianized version of Psalm 51.) "This expression," The Patriarch continues, "does not appear in the Septuagint nor in those other [translations] nor in the Hebrew [text]; but that Hebrew said to me: 'We have here found more than two hundred Psalms of David among our books' . . . I have, however, received from them no answer to my letter on these points, and I have no suitable person whom I can send. This is as fire in my heart, burning and blazing in my bones." The passages the Patriarch inquired about can hardly be expected to turn up among the Dead Sea documents. They are obviously of Christian origin, and the literature of Christianity probably did not begin to be written down till after the destruction of the monastery. But the ninth-century searchers of the caves might well have found in *The Book of Enoch* the prophecy invoked by Jude as well as—in a work that, as we shall later see, turned up among the first lot of scrolls—a good many unknown psalms.

The letter of the ninth-century patriarch, taken

in conjunction with the recent finds, throws light on another mystery. There was founded at Bagdad, in the eighth Christian century, an heretical Jewish sect, who rejected the authority of the Talmud and renewed the direct contact with the Bible. This sect, who called themselves Karaites, still exists in the East, and, before the Revolution, survived in Russia. Now, the literature of the Karaites is full of references to the Zadokite sect, and one of the Karaite authors says that the Zadokite fragments from Cairo, the *manuscript* of which has been assigned to some date in the Middle Ages, was actually found among Karaite books. The Karaites invoked these writings, says J. L. Teicher of Cambridge, who has especially studied this aspect of the subject, "to demonstrate the lineage of their creed by reference to the documents of an ancient opposition to Talmudic Judaism." And he believes that their peculiar calendar, their dietary rules and some other customs were inspired by the literature of the sect. But why does the characteristic language of the sect turn up suddenly in the ninth century without having played any part in earlier post-Christian Jewish literature? Because, Dr. Teicher answers, the Zadokite writings had just been discovered in the cave that the Patriarch heard about. His letter must, of course, have been written before either he or his correspondent died— that is, sometime in the last half of the eighth or very early in the ninth century. Teicher says that the peculiar forms of the script of the Dead Sea manuscripts also suddenly begin to appear in Hebrew documents of the tenth century. It has further been noticed by Père de Vaux that one of the Karaite authors, writing about 937 A.D., tells of an ancient sect, which he seems to assign to the same general period as the Sadducees and Jesus, who are called the Magharites because their books have been found in a cave (*magharah* in Arabic means *cave*); and the same sect is also mentioned by two later Muslem writers, one of whom says that it flourished in the middle of the first century B.C.

Thus today a whole set of documents, never before understood in relation to one another, seem perfectly to fall into place and acquire a new significance as belonging to the literature of the Dead Sea sect or representing, in some earlier or later phase, the tendencies it represents. There takes shape a whole missing chapter for the history of the growth of religious ideas between Judaism and Christianity—a chapter which, as Albright has said in his Postscript of 1951 to Brownlee's translation of the Manual of Discipline, "bids fair to revolutionize our approach to the beginnings of Christianity." "Rabbinical studies," he adds, "are even more directly affected, and it is safe to say that nothing written on the sectarian movements of the last three centuries of the Second Temple can escape thorough revision in the light of the evidence now available and still to be published." More recently,

in a review in the *Herald Tribune* book supplement
of July 18, 1954, he has said that it will now "be
necessary to rewrite all our New Testament
background material, since the new sources fill an
almost total blank in Jewish literature between the
latest apocrypha and the earliest rabbinical sources."
One may cite here, also, the opinion of one of the
leading French Hebrew scholars, M. André Dupont-
Sommer of the Sorbonne, who has published two
books on the scrolls. Of the hitherto so puzzling
literature of the pre-Christian apocrypha, he writes
in the first of these books: "All questions of literary
and historical criticism relative to this literature
must be entirely reconsidered. We are confronted
with a whole mass of documents the historical study
of which presented extreme difficulties, since so
many of the allusions they contained remained for
the most part indecipherable. But now the religious
history of the last two centuries before our era has
been illuminated by new light; a thousand details in
the writings of this period now become intelligible,
emerging at last from chaos."

I have mentioned the apocryphal documents of
the "intertestamental" period which were already
known in translations before the discovery of the
Dead Sea scrolls. In connection with these scattered
writings, it was long ago fully realized that they
belonged to a transitional literature between Judaism and Christianity. The invocation of the Saviour-
Messiah becomes more important and pressing than

it has been in the canonical books; and the new writings more and more take the form of apocalypses —that is, of supernatural visions which reveal past, present and future under the guise of a phantasmagoria of symbolic persons and animals, divine and diabolical beings, celestial and infernal phenomena. The situation is summed up by Charles in his introduction to the second volume of his great edition of the apocrypha. The Judaic Law of the Pentateuch had come, he says, by the third pre-Christian century to be conceived "as the final and supreme revelation of God . . . there was now no longer room for independent representatives of God appearing before men, such as the pre-Exilic prophets." According to Zechariah (13:15), writing about 300 B.C. from the conservative priestly point of view, a man could be, or ought to be, put to death for setting himself up as a prophet. The result of this was that a writer who had had a new revelation was forced to ascribe his account of it either to one of the canonical prophets or to one of the pentateuchal patriarchs. The late apocryphal writings are put forth, in many cases, as the utterances of Enoch or Moses, Jeremiah, Baruch or Isaiah. One such work, the Book of Daniel, got into the regular canon, though—in the Hebrew Bible, not the Christian one—it was not admitted to the company of the Prophets but relegated to the section of miscellaneous Sacred Writings. This work, which purports to deal with events of the Babylonian

Captivity, is actually meant to apply to the struggles of the Jews of the Hellenic period against their Seleucid king, Antiochus Epiphanes, and it contains, in Daniel's visions and Nebuchadnezzar's dreams, the first extensive examples of the apocalypse in its characteristic form. The problem for the scholar or historian was to work out the correspondences between the fantastic happenings described in this apocalyptic literature and actual recorded events; and this task is made rather difficult by the tendency of Jewish writers to see everything from the standpoint of God: lacking our Western historical sense, they mix up past, present and future and refer to contemporary persons under the names of legendary figures.

Now, two of the first lot of scrolls belong to this apocalyptic type. One of these—the one that Professor Sukenik described to the correspondents in the midst of the Arab shellfire—was called by him *The War of the Children of Light against the Children of Darkness*. (This has hithero been known only in passages to the authorities I here rely on, since Professor Sukenik died before he had finished editing it. The whole of the Hebrew text has only just been brought out by his son, General Yigael Yadin.) The other of these unknown works represents a special variation, itself hitherto unknown, on the familiar apocalyptic form. Ostensibly a commentary, verse by verse, on the canonical prophet Habakkuk, it is in reality a history of happenings that were recent at the time it was written but that are chronicled here in terms of the assumption that Habakkuk was prophesying them. (This was a genre which had not been known when the first lot of scrolls was found, but among the more recently found manuscripts, some fragments have now been identified as belonging to a similar interpretation of Micah.) Both these documents deal with a war, and in both cases the enemy are called the Kittim. Kittim is a name which originally and properly meant the people of Kition, a city in Cyprus, but it was later applied by the Jews, with their still rather dim ideas of their Mediterranean neighbours, to the Eastern Islands in general, to Macedonia, and even to Italy. In *The War of the Children of Light*, we hear of the "Kittim of Asshur," evidently the Syrians, the Seleucids, and the "Kittim of Egypt," evidently the followers of the Ptolemies. In the Habakkuk Commentary, they are simply the Kittim, but their practices and methods are described with a certain amount of particularity; we are told that they are "swift and valiant in battle," that they are "a source of terror . . . to all the nations," that they are "insolent toward the mighty" and "mock at kings and chiefs," that they "scorn the fortresses of the people" and "surround them" and "lay them in ruins", that their captains "take command" and then "disappear one after the other," that they plunder the people they conquer and afterwards saddle them with taxes, and that they "put many to the sword, young men, adults, old men, women and children, and have no pity for the fruit of the womb." All this would appear to apply to the Romans better than to anyone else. The disappearance of the leaders one after the other might well describe the situation that prevailed during the Civil Wars when consuls and generals were always being changed. The fact that the Kittim are also said to "devour all the nations like an eagle" would be equally appropriate for the Romans, whose standards had eagles on them; and the identification would seem to be clinched by the custom attributed to this enemy of "sacrificing to their standards". "Their arms," says the author of the Commentary, "are themselves the object of their religion." The cult of the battle *signa* among the Roman legions is attested by a number of ancient writers. Though all scholars do not agree in identifying the Kittim with the Romans, the conclusions of General Yadin, in a study of *The War of the Children of Light*, would seem to confirm this hypothesis. He believes that certain weapons assigned to the enemy are to be recognized as Roman short swords, and that many of the military details of the conflict described in this scroll can only apply, or would best apply, to the period of Julius Caesar. The Kittim of Asshur and the Kittim of Egypt would be Syrians and Egyptians allied with them.

M. Dupont-Sommer, whose arguments I have summarized above, believes that the Commentary

was most probably written in the year 41 B.C.—
that is, three years after Julius Caesar's death. He
has also attempted to identify in it two figures who
are never named and who are evidently of great
importance in the history of the Dead Sea sect.
One of these is a Teacher of Righteousness, a priest
who has been favoured with divine revelations and
who is the leader of a community, a party, the
members of which are poor and who call themselves
"the New Covenant." The teacher is referred to as
the Elect of God. He insists on the strictest observance of the Law, yet is at odds with the priests of
Jerusalem. He has been persecuted by a Wicked
Priest, sometimes, apparently, referred to as the
Prophet of Untruth or the Man of Untruth, who
has "swallowed him up in the heat of his anger,"
has "dared to strip him of his clothing," and has
struck him "in the execution of iniquitous judg-
ments," when "odious profaners have committed
horrors on him and vengeance on the body of
flesh." (I am following Dupont-Sommers' rendering.
Other scholars translate these passages differently.
I shall return to this problem later.) But the
persecutors are to be punished: "so, at the end of the
festival, on the resting of the Day of Atonement, he
[the Teacher of Righteousness] appeared in splen-
dour unto them for the purpose of swallowing them
up, and that they might stumble on that fast day,
the sabbath of their resting." (This rendering is
Brownlee's, as are those that follow.) And we are

told that the Wicked Priest, "in the sight of the Teacher of Righteousness and the men of his counsel," has been given by God "into the hand of his enemies to abuse with smiting that he might be consumed with bitterness of soul, because he has done evil against His elect."

Who is this Teacher of Righteousness, and who is this Wicked Priest? I have spoken of the close similarities between the Manual of Discipline and the Zadokite fragments. A new link in the chain of evidence was supplied when it was noted that the Teacher of Righteousness also figured in the Zadokite work (the phrase is exactly the same save for the omission in the latter of the article), and that in both cases his followers are said to be bound by a Covenant or New Covenant. The word "covenant", furthermore, is used throughout the Manual of Discipline in referring to the members of the order. It will also be seen from the description above of the followers of the Teacher of Righteousness that this, too, coincides with the picture put together from Josephus and Philo. The Prophet of Untruth and the Man of Untruth both appear in the Zadokite fragments, and the Prophet of Untruth is mentioned in the fragments of the Micah commentary. M. Dupont-Sommer assumes that both these are names for the Wicked Priest, and he finds in Josephus a figure whose role seems to correspond with what we are told about this hated man. This is Aristobulus II, one of the Jewish Hasmonean dynasty, high priest of Jerusalem as well as king, who ruled over the Jewish state for three and a half years (between 67 and 63); who was arrested in 63 and imprisoned by Pompey at Rome; who escaped and returned to Palestine but was caught and sent back in irons—so that he must have been forced, "in bitterness of soul," to take part in Pompey's triumph; and who was finally, in 49, poisoned in prison by Pompey's supporters. There is one striking piece of evidence in favour of this identification. The Commentary speaks of "the house of Absalom and the men of their counsel, who were silent at the reproof of the Teacher of Righteousness and did not help him against the Man of Untruth, who had rejected the Law among all peoples." Now, we know from Josephus that Aristobulus had an uncle named Absalom and had married his daughter.

As for the Teacher of Righteousness, this may have been a general title that was given to a succession of Messiahs. Before the discovery of the Dead Sea scrolls, the earliest known reference to the Messiah as "The Elect One" and "The Righteous One" occurred in *The Book of Enoch*—which Charles assigned to the early years of the first B.C. century; and not only do these names appear in the literature of the Dead Sea sect, they are applied in the Gospels to Jesus—as is the phrase "the Son of Man," which, though common in the Old Testament prophets, is first applied to the Messiah in

88

*Enoch.* There were certainly several persons accepted as Messiahs by various writers in various situations; yet these documents from the Dead Sea cave do seem to refer to a specific man. A number of suggestions have been advanced, and Josephus has again been consulted, together with Second Maccabees, in both of which is found the story of a high priest of Jerusalem called Onias, exemplary in his "godliness" and "hatred of wickedness," who was first supplanted by his brother, then murdered by the successor of that brother. But this was under the Seleucids; Onias was put to death in 171 B.C. In this event, the Dead Sea monastery would first have been occupied (136?) some twenty-five years later than the murder of the Teacher of Righteousness, and the sect would have had time to abandon the custom of animal sacrifices, which Onias, as High Priest, would of course have had to observe, and to have adopted their periodical calendar (first described in *The Book of Jubilees,* which has been dated by R. H. Charles between 153 and 105 B.C.). In this case, the Wicked Priest would be the High Priest Menelaus, of whom we are told in Second Maccabees that "he came to Jerusalem, bringing nothing worthy the high priesthood, but having the passion of a cruel tyrant and the rage of a savage beast." He is also, like the Wicked Priest, described as a monster of rapacity. It is evident that Onias' murder much shocked the Jewish world, and it has long been supposed that

the reference in the ninth chapter of Daniel (165
B.C.?) to a Messiah of whom it is prophesied that
he shall "be cut off" and "have nothing," applies
to the murder of Onias. But then what becomes of
the theory nailed down by Dupont-Sommer with
the reference to the House of Absalom and the worship of the Roman standards? Since no other personal name is mentioned, this Absalom may be
merely the Absalom of the Bible, invoked in a
symbolic sense for Joseph, a nephew of Onias, who
robbed him of much of his authority; and how do
we know that the Seleucid armies did not worship
their standards, too? It was one of Dupont-Sommer's points that the Kittim of the Commentary
cannot be the Syrians, since the Syrians would not
be said to come from the "isles" of the sea, but it
has been objected to this that the word translated
*isles* is a vague one, which may be used for any
maritime region, and that if the Kittim could be
Macedonians, they might just as well be Syrians—
especially in view of the fact that in *The War of the
Children of Light* it is quite plain that the Kittim are
Seleucids. And if the Wicked Priest was Menelaus,
may not the Man of Untruth have been a different
person?—Antiochus Epiphanes perhaps. M.
Dupont-Sommer himself entertains an inverse
hypothesis: that the names, although interchange-
able, may both apply to two people: Aristobulus II
and his brother who succeeded him, Hyrcanus II.
The situation has been complicated further by

certain scholars' calling attention to the possibility
that, from the point where a shift is made in the
verb-forms of the Habakkuk Commentary, the
events alluded to may belong to the domain of
prophecy—that is, may be merely predicted because
they are strongly desired. (In his account of *The
War of the Children of Light against the Children of
Darkness*, the editor, General Yadin, describes it as
an ideal vision of a triumph which was still in the
future, but one which was presented in terms of
actual Hebrew weapons, strategy and ritual tactics.)

Dr. W. H. Brownlee believes that the whole story
involved in the Habakkuk Commentary is supposed
to be told by the Teacher of Righteousness, and
that he is made to predict for the future the events
that followed his death. Dr. Brownlee also believes
that *three* Wicked Priests are referred to—Alexander
Jannaeus, Aristobulus II and Hyrcanus II; and he
discovers a succession of clues for identifying them
in this chronological order. He suggests that the
Teacher of Righteousness may be a certain Judah
mentioned in the Talmud, who is said to have
rebuked Hyrcanus I. He explains that when he
published his translation of the Habakkuk Commentary (quoted above), he had assumed that it
was the Wicked Priest who "reproved" the Teacher
of Righteousness, but that the text may be read
also the other way; he finds in Josephus an Essene
named Judas (the Hellenized form of Judah), who

instructed his disciples in the art of prophecy and who was evidently opposed to the official priesthood. Now, among the three scrolls from the original cave that were acquired by Professor Sukenik is a collection of thirty-five psalms—hitherto completely unknown—which have been called the "Thanksgiving Hymns." (The complete text of these hymns has now at last been published by the Hebrew University in Jerusalem; only five of them up to this time were generally available to scholars.) These are thought to have been composed either by the Teacher of Righteousness himself or, in honour of him, by a disciple who acts as the prophet's mouthpiece. Dr. Brownlee points out that each one of them begins with the phrase, "I will praise thee, O Lord," and that these were the words of Leah when Judah, her fourth son, was born. The author of these psalms, says Yadin, "speaks eloquently of his persecution and of the persecution of his people, and then, for more than twenty pages gives thanks, in majestic language, for his deliverance from his enemies." But we do not know whether this deliverance has actually taken place or is merely being predicted with certainty. Although you have, here again, descriptions of weapons and tactics of war, you have no clear historical data.

I have indicated here, in the most simplified form, only three of the lines of theory that have been worked out by various scholars to elucidate the Habakkuk Commentary. The literature of the subject is enormous, and it is impossible to summarize it briefly. I have tried merely to give some idea of the difficulty of determining the actual events—and one cannot always be sure they *are* actual—that are dealt with in these late Hebrew writings; of accommodating apocalyptic visions to the more realistic chronicles of such Hellenized Jews as Josephus and the author of Second Maccabees. But if definite events and the actors in them are hard to pin down as history, the doctrines and the mystical symbols are not so easily to be mistaken. These are not in all cases consistent—they must belong to a religious movement that extended through some two and a half centuries; but it is obvious that a certain theology not only runs through all this group of late apocryphal documents and the literature of the Dead Sea sect, but extends to the New Testament, also. It will not be possible here to trace the whole intricate web of cross-references and interrelations that threads these writings together. I shall have to confine myself to describing the principal elements of this school of Messianic thought.

One of its most important doctrines, then, is the morality of the Two Ways, quite unknown to the ancient Hebrews, that appears in so many of these documents. One finds in this literature again and again the Way of Darkness and the Way of Light, the Spirit of Darkness and the Spirit of Light, the Children of Darkness and the Children of Light.

The Light is Truth, and the Darkness Falsehood. The Messiah, the Teacher of Righteousness, is opposed to a Demon of Evil, most frequently known as Belial or Beliar. The Way of Good leads to salvation; the Way of Evil to torment. There is to be a Last Judgment at the end of time—equally unknown to ancestral Judaism—when the Messiah shall divide the world. He, the Elect One, shall save the Elect, the people of the New Covenant. The wrongs they have suffered at the hands of their enemies will finally be avenged. But, in the meantime, they must keep themselves holy by means of the sacred repasts, presided over by a priest, purgation by baptism and constant washings. There are three references in the Zadokite fragments to the "well of living water" that saves, which seem to anticipate the conversation of Jesus with the woman of Samaria at the well, when he speaks of the "spring of water welling up to eternal life," and the several New Testament passages that associate baptism both with such Old Testament references as those of Jeremiah to God as a "fountain of living waters" and with spiritual regeneration through Christ. The living waters of Jeremiah are a metaphor, but it seems clear that the water of the Zadokite fragments, taken in conjunction with what we know of the ceremonies of the sect, is something more than a metaphor. We find, for example, in the Manual of Discipline the following significant passage: "And then God will purge by His truth all the deeds of man, refining for himself some of mankind in order to abolish every evil spirit from the midst of his flesh, and to cleanse him through a Holy Spirit from all wicked practices, sprinkling upon him a spirit of truth as purifying water to cleanse him from all untrue abominations and from wallowing in [or, being defiled by] the spirit of impurity— so as to give the upright insight into the knowledge of the Most High and into the wisdom of the sons of Heaven, to give the perfect way of understanding." It may be, as I have mentioned above, that baptism as well as sun-worship, had already reached Palestine from the East—as the doctrine of the Two Spirits of Zarathustra, and the later Persian theology of Manichaeism that regarded the world as the object of a struggle between two spirits of Light-Good and Darkness-Evil, which existed independently of one another, instead of as the work of an omnipotent God who had created both Good and Evil—a religion which, originating in the third A.D. century, for a time gave Christianity some fairly severe competition.

The doctrine of the Two Ways is found, however, in a document that has become a part of Christian literature yet has always remained rather mysterious. Before this document was actually discovered, it had been known, from the ancient lists of canonical and non-canonical writings, that there had once existed a work called the *Didachē*, or *Teaching of the Twelve Apostles*. It had also been suspected that some work, referred to by scholars as *The Two Ways*, had been used and partly incorporated into a number of early church manuals and writings of the apostolic fathers. In 1882, the German Catholic scholar Adam Krawutzcky attempted a reconstruction of *The Two Ways*, and it is one of the dramatic accidents of scholarship that in the very next year, 1883, a newly found Greek text of the *Didachē* should have been published by a Greek Metropolitan of Constantinople—a text that began "There are two ways . . ." and the first section of which was obviously the unknown work that Krawutzcky had been trying to reconstruct. His guesses were confirmed to an astonishing extent. The next year, a fragment of a Latin version of what was clearly the same document was also brought to light, and it was seen that this did not contain the specifically Christian references that were a feature of the Greek *Didachē*. It was now thought by certain scholars that *The Two Ways*—I quote from the eleventh edition of the Encyclopaedia Britannica— "had the appearance of being a Jewish manual which had been carried over into the use of the Christian Church." "But this," the Britannica adds, "is of course only a probable inference; there is no prototype extant in Jewish literature." There can be now, however, little doubt as to the source not only of *The Two Ways* but also of the second part of the *Didachē*, which is a manual of church ordinances. You have here, just as you have in the

Manual of Discipline of the Dead Sea monastery,
the two ways of light and of darkness that lead
respectively to life and to death, and that are
presided over each by its angel, and you have, also,
the similar language of the "strife" that goes on
between them and the "crown" that the good man
may win. You have the baptism (in the *Didachē*,
preceded by fasting), which we know to have been
fundamental to the ritual of the sect, and you have
a sacred repast, which involves broken bread and a
cup of wine, but at which the wine represents "the
Holy Vine of Thy [God's] son David," and the
bread the "life and knowledge which Thou didst
make known to us through Jesus, Thy child."
Note that, though Jesus is mentioned here, there is
nothing about the Christian atonement. It had
sometimes been believed hitherto that the ceremony
of the bread and the wine in the Gospel accounts of
the Last Supper was based on the blessing of the
bread and wine in the Jewish celebration of the
Passover, but Professor Karl Georg Kuhn, of
Göttingen, has pointed out, in a study of the
development of the Eucharist, that the Passover
ceremony is a family affair, at which both men and
women are present and at which the father presides,
whereas the primitive Christian Communion, in the
tradition of the Last Supper, had for participants
only men, who were the members of a limited
circle, and was presided over by the head of a
congregation. We have seen that the banquets

of the sect were sacred and a very important part of its ritual. Professor Kuhn believes that the Christian Communion derives from these, and that the atonement was introduced into it by Jesus himself. But this is not, as we have seen, in the *Didachē*, and others believe that it was introduced later.

The discovery, among the fragments found in the first Qumrân cave, of two missing columns of the Manual of Discipline which had not been published when Dr. Kuhn wrote, increases the plausibility of this theory that the ritual of the Last Supper ultimately derives from the sect. A procedure is here prescribed which has even more striking resemblances to that of the Christian Communion. Whenever as many as ten shall gather together for a banquet, they shall take their seats in order of precedence, and the priest and the Messiah shall preside. The company may not touch the bread and the wine till the priest has blessed them and taken some—after which the Messiah first takes some, then the others in order of rank. It may be that the ceremony here described is a liturgical anticipation of a banquet expected in Heaven, that the Messiah is not actually present but that the priest is acting in his name, as the Christian priest does for Christ. It has also been suggested that an incident in Luke's description of the Last Supper has a significance which can only be understood in connection with the ritual of the Manual: "A dispute arose among them as to which of them should be regarded as the greatest. And he [Jesus] said to them, The kings of the Gentiles exercise lordship over them; and those in authority over them are called benefactors. But not so with you; rather let the greatest among you become as the youngest, and the leader as one who serves." We do not know what the relation of Jesus to the Essene order was, but it sounds as if, on this occasion, he were deliberately upsetting its protocol. We have learned from Josephus how rigid, among the members of the sect, was the hierarchy based on seniority, and the language of "greatest" and "youngest" is very much what we get in the Manual, which talks about "greater" and "lesser."

The resemblances between the Manual and the *Didachē* have been carefully traced by a Catholic priest, Père Jean-Paul Audet, who has also published in *La Revue Biblique* a study, from the same point of view, of another once supposedly Christian work, the *Shepherd* of Hermas (both subjects are covered in the papers that have appeared under the general title *Affinités Littéraires et Doctrinales du 'Manuel de Discipline'*). This is a book of "Visions, Mandates, and Similitudes," written about the middle of the second Christian century, which was long accepted in certain quarters as a part of the Christian canon but was relegated at the end of the fifth century, through the action of a council of the Roman Church, to a non-canonical status. This book has always been found rather puzzling.

Though a Son of God figures in it, he is never referred to as Jesus or Christ, and neither he nor a Holy Spirit who is also occasionally mentioned behaves as one would expect them to do in conformity with Christian theology. Père Audet now rereads the *Shepherd* in the light of these recent discoveries. It has always, he says, been hard to account for it precisely because scholars have approached it from the point of view of what it is *not*—that is, in relation to Christianity. If one looks at it from the point of view of what it *is*, one sees that it is perfectly in order as a product of the doctrines of the brotherhood. The God, the Son of God and the Holy Spirit of Hermas do not constitute a Trinity: it is God who dominates the *Shepherd*; the son and the spirit are mentioned only in special connections. The "Church" of which Hermas speaks does not owe its establishment to the "Son of God"; it had already a long history behind it when the latter was sent to purify it and to recall it to God's commandments; it has not even been founded by men. "Something," says Père Audet, "has dictated in a positive way the unity of Hermas' theological thought, and something must also have determined its quality." This something is a Judaic, not a Christian tradition, but a Judaic tradition of a particular kind that now for the first time becomes recognizable. Hermas mentions the *Didachē*, which is evidently one of the sources of his "Mandates"; and you find again in the *Shepherd* the Way of

Darkness and the Way of Light that lead to salvation or perdition, and, again, the two angels assigned to them. You find the atonement by baptism, and this is the only kind of atonement mentioned. As for the Holy Spirit, we have seen, in the passage just quoted from the Manual, that a Holy Spirit was associated with the ritual of cleansing by baptism, and this seems to be the same Holy Spirit that twice figures in the Zadokite fragments as something that must not be defiled. Now, Hermas tells us that he lived in Rome, and that he had been at one time a slave. The guess has been hazarded by Père Audet that his father had been a Jew who belonged to the Dead Sea sect, and that, after the descent of the Romans in 70 A.D. (when the monastery was probably destroyed), he brought the boy to Rome and sold him. ("He who brought me up," writes Hermas, "sold me to a certain Rhoda at Rome.") The son would eventually have become a Christian, but would already have been so deeply imbued with the doctrine in its older form that he would never have really assimilated the theology elaborated by the Christians.

# 5

## *What would Renan have said?*

As soon as one sets out to study the controversies provoked by the Dead Sea scrolls, one becomes aware of a certain "tension." "During the past three years," wrote Dr. Albright in 1951, "there has been a debate about the chronology of the scrolls which has at times attained the status of a veritable *guerre des savants*. It is an astounding chapter in the history of learning, in some ways without parallel." But the tension does not all arise from the at first much disputed problems of dating, and the contention about the dating itself had, perhaps, behind it other anxieties than the purely scholarly ones.

The elements of the situation, of which I was already though vaguely aware, were pointed up for me in a piquant manner by an evening I spent in Israeli Jerusalem with a distinguished Jewish scholar from Prague, Mr. David Flusser. I had just read, in the *Israel Exploration Journal*, an interesting paper by Flusser, connecting still another apocryphal book, the so-called *Ascension of Isaiah*, with the Dead Sea literature. In examining the section of this book known as *The Martyrdom of Isaiah*, which is supposed to be pre-Christian, Dr. Flusser was led to suspect that the Old Testament prophet had here been made to stand for the Teacher of Righteousness. The opponent of Isaiah here is Belial, the Angel of Lawlessness, whom—since Belial, as we have seen, is the characteristic name given, in this group of writings, to the ruler of the forces of evil—Flusser identifies with the Angel of Darkness, ruler of "all the sons of lawlessness," who figures in the Manual of Discipline; as well as with the Angel of Darkness and Evil of the Two Ways of the *Didachē*. This Isaiah is sawed in two by the human agents of Belial for saying that he has seen God— which Moses had expressly said it was impossible to do and live—and that he now knows more than Moses. (The Habakkuk Commentary asserts that God had made known to the Teacher of Righteousness "all the secrets of the words of his servants the prophets.") But just before Isaiah's martyrdom, he has spoken to his followers and told them to "flee away" to the region of Tyre and Sidon: "For me only has God mixed the cup." There is no mention in the Bible or elsewhere of a flight to Tyre and Sidon; but Flusser calls attention to the following passage in the Zadokite fragments: "All those who turned back were delivered to the sword, and those who held fast escaped into the land of the north." Damascus and Tyre and Sidon were all to the north of Jerusalem, and all, in both Seleucid and Roman times, belonged to the same department of imperial administration. It is Flusser's conjecture that the author of *The Martyrdom of Isaiah* "took part in the controversy over this departure" and "tried to prove by the authority of the prophet Isaiah that the departure was prefigured according to the Divine Will."

This theory, though not implausible, is hardly supported by such evidence as seems to be quite conclusive in tying together the other documents. But Flusser is a learned and intelligent man, who is very much worth listening to on the subject of the scrolls, with which, though this is not his field, he has recently been occupying himself. I had met him in the library of the University and asked him to come to see me, and he arrived at the King David Hotel, precipitately, abruptly, hatless, with his briefcase in his hand, and the moment we sat down in the lobby, quite without a conventional opening —since he knew that I was looking for light on the subject—he began to talk about the scrolls. He was dynamic, imaginative, passionately interested. I had heard about his absorption in ancient texts—which he seems always to carry about him—while waiting in queues for his marketing. The important thing, he said at once, was not the polemics about the dates, but what was implied by the contents of the manuscripts. He started in English but asked if he could speak French. His English was bad; and few people understood Czech. (I had the impression that German was not often spoken in Israel.) Hebrew he had learned, he added, rather late in life; "My best language here is really medieval Latin." I knew that he was primarily a student of medieval subjects, but asked him with whom he spoke Latin. "With the Jesuits," he replied. I had been told that if you asked him a question, it would take him three hours to answer, and I could see now what people meant, but he was neither a bore nor garrulous. On the contrary, I have rarely known a scholar who expressed himself—with all his material at his fingertips—so brilliantly and so much to the point. He would give me, to each of my questions, a full and closely reasoned answer, and stop when he had covered the ground. All the texts that were needed he had brought in his briefcase, and he handed me a Greek Testament for me to follow the Pauline Epistles while he held before me the Hebrew texts and translated them fluently into Greek, demonstrating that not only the doctrine but the language itself was exactly the same. I do not remember now the passages he read, but one of them must have been the description of baptism from the Manual of Discipline, quoted above, which might well have been juxtaposed to the Epistle to Titus, 3:5: "Not by works of righteousness which we have done, but according to his mercy he saved us, by the washing of regeneration, and renewal in the Holy Spirit." On the doctrine of Election, of salvation by grace, that is implied in such a statement and that dominates the Pauline Epistles, Mr. Flusser talked with much animation. "For the doctrine of Election," he said, "we have now a new genealogy: the Teacher of Righteousness, Paul, Spinoza, Calvin, Hegel, Marx—one of the most disastrous of human ideas, the doctrine of predestination!" Such were the pressure and tempo of Mr. Flusser's talk that he was carried at one point to lengths that had no parallel in my experience of even the most enthusiastic talkers. Not only did he raise his voice, when some insight had taken possession of him, quite oblivious of the people sitting near us and as if he were lecturing in a classroom, but when, at the climax of one of his arguments—though we had tried to get away from the orchestra by going to the farthest corner—the music impinged on our conversation, my companion, caught up by a familiar tune, actually sang a few bars of his exposition, as if it were part of an opera; then pulled himself up and returned to prose, as he put his text back in the briefcase.

I was already beginning to realize the explosive possibilities of the subject, and I now heard these described with candour. "*Les chrétiens sont dérangés,*" Mr. Flusser declared. "*Les juifs sont dérangés aussi. Moi, je ne suis pas dérangé!*" It had already been made very clear to me at the Hebrew University that the sect had "grown up inside Judaism, but had nothing to do with Judaism," and I had seemed to note, also, on the Christian side, a certain reluctance to recognize that the characteristic doctrines of Christianity must have been developed gradually and naturally, in the course of a couple of hundred years, out of a dissident branch of Judaism. This was what was upsetting to the scholars, who were mostly, on the Christian side, either Anglican divines, Roman Catholic priests or Presbyterian or Methodist Ministers, and, on the Jewish side, if not Orthodox Jews, at least specialists in the literature of Judaism, who approached it with a certain piety. An independent scholar like Flusser, not committed to any religion, had no reason for being upset. *"C'est très désagréable pour tout le monde,"* he said to me on another occasion,—*"sauf pour ceux qui s'occupent des apocalypses—ils sont contents."* He seemed even to regard it as a little risky to come to grips publicly and boldly with the implications of the scrolls; but he enjoyed his informed detachment, and there were moments when I almost felt that the Devil had sent him to Jerusalem to make the most of the situation. Mr. Flusser is a short stocky man, with sharp little cold green eyes that glint behind rimless glasses, under modestly Mephistophelian eyebrows, and red hair that stands straight up from his forehead. And he delights in deadpan humour, which, if one does not show signs at once of appre-

ciating his ironic intent, he underlines with a harsh
dry laugh. I have seen him disconcert other scholars
by insisting that the errors in sacred texts and the
ignorant misreadings of them were really the con-
structive element in the history of civilization, since
the religious ideas that have had most success have
mainly been founded upon them. Yet Flusser is
much respected, and his scholarly work is quite
sober; nor has he anything of the polymath's
*blasement*. I joined him, when we later removed to the
bar, in a toast to what he called "*le vrai saint esprit*"
—the πνεῦμα ἅγιον and רוח הקדש had been
flitting about our corner of the lobby—that hum-
anity carries with it. And he talked to me with
admiration of the character of the Teacher of Righteousness, of which he felt he had been able to form
some idea through reading the whole of the text
of the then still unpublished *Thanksgiving Hymns*: a
courageous man, he believed, who had lived his
defeat with dignity. There was nothing of Jesus,
said Flusser, in the morality of the Teacher of
Righteousness, for Jesus had taught people to love
their enemies, and the Teacher felt nothing but
hatred for his and expected the Lord to avenge him.
Nor was there anything, he pointed out, in the
doctrine of the Teacher's followers, of the Christian
idea that salvation is to be gained by believing
in Jesus, who will take all our sins away.

I later attended with Flusser and two younger
Israeli scholars an evening session of lectures

devoted to the Dead Sea scrolls. At dinner, he provoked a protest by announcing that, since the function of apologetics was fundamental to science, he did not object to apologetics. He went on, disregarding objections, to explain that, in spite of this, he always distrusted people who, like one of the speakers on the programme, invariably began by explaining that their opinions were quite objective and did not represent special pleading. This session on the scrolls was interesting. The speeches, which were all in Hebrew, were translated to me by one of my other companions. The inhibitions of the Jews in regard to the scrolls were brought out by a well-known Israeli scholar, Mr. A. M. Habermann, who said that the Jewish scholars had sometimes been shy of these documents, for fear of their destroying the authority of the Masoretic text of the Bible, and that they sometimes took the attitude —which the speaker regretted—that the subject was of less interest to Jews than to Christians. Yet the large auditorium was packed. It was the Passover holidays, and this evening session was merely one feature of a week of lectures especially given for teachers, many of them from out of town, who seemed to attend these sessions in preference to other entertainment. They began at, I think, half past eight in the morning and went on till eleven at night. All were on Biblical subjects. I had the impression that these talks on the scrolls were of special interest to the audiences; and when Flusser,

who had also spoken, came back at the end to
join us, he exclaimed, in a terrific pun—*megillot*
is the Hebrew word for *scrolls*: "*Tout le monde est
mégillotmane!*"

The next morning I crossed over to Jordan, where
I stayed, in Old Jerusalem, at the American School
of Oriental Research. Dr. Frank M. Cross, Jr., of
the McCormick Theological Seminary in Chicago,
who was working on the new material, was Annual
Professor at the School; and the resident director
was Dr. James Muilenburg of Union Theological
Seminary, who had been studying some new
fragments of Ecclesiastes, and had come to the
conclusion that this pessimistic and rather sophisti-
cated book cannot have been written so late as has
been supposed by some, but must belong to the
third or fourth, rather than to the second, pre-
Christian century. These last years—with their
findings of Egyptian tombs, the excavations of
Paestum, Pompeii and Athens, the plumbing of the
millenial layers of Jericho and the deciphering at
last of the Minoan script—have been a heyday for
archaeologists; and the excavation of the monastery,
the reading of the Dead Sea manuscripts, have been
followed with intense eagerness. It seemed to me
very regrettable that the barrier between Israel and
Jordan should be cutting off from one another the
two groups of Semitic scholars who—in the Jordan
Museum in Old Jerusalem and at the Hebrew University in New—have been working on, respectively,

the new harvest of fragments and the three
Sukenik manuscripts. The people at the University
know nothing of de Vaux's discoveries except what
they learn at long intervals from the reports in *La
Revue Biblique* (a quarterly published in Paris, but
edited by de Vaux from Jerusalem), and they must
wait for the texts to be brought out in instalments—
which will mean a matter of years—by the Oxford
University Press. At the same time, till the very
recent publication of the Hebrew University texts,
the Christian scholar had no access to them. In
Israel, at the session the night before, I had listened
to an expert in rabbinics, a tall, lean, black-
bearded man, wearing a flat-topped black cap, who
looked like a rabbi himself, explaining—from a
study of the photographs of the complete Isaiah
scroll then in the United States—that it showed
every evidence of having been executed in strict
conformity with rabbinical rules. But no scholar
with this kind of competence can examine the newly
found manuscripts, for no Jew is admitted to Jordan
and no Jew known to be such is left there. Thus the
enmity between Jew and Arab is contributing to the
obstacles and touchiness of this curious situation,
which has also been a little affected by the rivalry
between Jews and Christians. You sometimes find
Jewish scholars implying that their Gentile oppon-
ents do not really know Hebrew well enough to
arrive at a sound opinion, and, on the other
side, non-Jewish Hebraists taking a lofty and off-

hand tone on the value of rabbinical studies.

The moment of maximum strain in the discussion of the Dead Sea documents may, perhaps, be fixed on the day—May 26, 1950—when M. Dupont-Sommer, Professor of Semitic Languages and Civilizations at the Sorbonne and Director of Studies at the Ecole des Hautes Etudes, read before the French Académie des Inscriptions et Belles-Lettres a paper on the Habakkuk Commentary. Dr. W. H. Brownlee, writing of this in the *Bulletin of the American Schools of Oriental Research* of December, 1953, refers to Dupont-Sommer as "the very original French orientalist," calls the paper "dramatic," and says that it "caused a sensation." "What evoked the most astonishment," Dr. Brownlee continued, "was his disclosure that the Teacher of Righteousness, founder of the sect of the scrolls, was in some respects an exact prototype of Jesus, particularly as a martyred prophet, revered by his followers as the suffering Servant of the Lord in Deutero-Isaiah." (Second Isaiah, the unknown author of the later chapters of the Book of Isaiah.)

Let us turn to Dupont-Sommer's own statement of his views in his book *Aperçus Préliminaires sur les Manuscrits de la Mer Morte* (translated under the title *The Dead Sea Scrolls: A Preliminary Survey*), published the same year that the paper was read.

"Everything in the Jewish New Covenant," says M. Dupont-Sommer, "heralds and prepares the way for the Christian New Covenant. The Galilean

Master, as He is presented to us in the writings of the
New Testament, appears in many respects as an
astonishing reincarnation of the Teacher of Righteousness. Like the latter, He preached penitence,
poverty, humility, love of one's neighbour, chastity.
Like him, He prescribed the observance of the
Law of Moses, the whole Law, but the Law finished
and perfected, thanks to His own revelations. Like
him, He was the Elect and the Messiah of God, the
Messiah redeemer of the world. Like him, He was
the object of the hostility of the priests, the party of
the Sadducees. Like him, He was condemned and
put to death. Like him, He pronounced judgment
on Jerusalem, which was taken and destroyed by
the Romans for having put Him to death. Like
him, at the end of time, He will be the supreme
judge. Like him, He founded a Church whose
adherents fervently awaited His glorious return. In
the Christian Church, just as in the Essene Church,
the essential rite is the sacred meal, whose ministers
are the priests. Here and there, at the head of each
community, there is the overseer, the 'bishop'.
And the ideal of both Churches is essentially that of
unity, communion in love—even going so far as the
sharing of common property.

"All these similarities—and here I only touch
upon the subject—taken together, constitute a very
impressive whole. The question at once arises, to
which of the two sects, the Jewish or the Christian,
does the priority belong? Which of the two was able

to influence the other? The reply leaves no room
for doubt. The Teacher of Righteousness died about
65-53 B.C.; Jesus the Nazarene died about 30 A.D.
In every case in which the resemblance compels or
invites us to think of a borrowing, this was on the
part of Christianity. But on the other hand, the
appearance of the faith in Jesus—the foundation of
the New Church—can scarcely be explained without
the real historic activity of a new Prophet, a new
Messiah, who has rekindled the flame and concen-
trated on himself the adoration of men."

These conclusions, Dr. Brownlee continued,
"aroused much opposition, partly inspired by the
fear that the uniqueness of Christ was at stake, but
securely grounded upon a careful study of the
texts adduced by Dupont-Sommer himself and
proving the tenuousness (if not impossibility) of the
constructions that he had placed upon them."

Indeed, if one examines the two passages of the
Habakkuk Commentary upon which M. Dupont-
Sommer mainly bases his theory that the Teacher of
Righteousness was martyred—I have given them,
in the section above, in Dupont-Sommer's own translation—one finds that they do not necessarily imply
this interpretation. In the one case, Habakkuk 2:7,
there is a gap of two lines, where the bottom of the
manuscript has been broken off, and it is the
translator who has filled this in with, "he [the
Wicked Priest] persecuted the Teacher of Righteousness." The context seems to make it more

probable that—as other translators have assumed—
it is the Wicked Priest himself upon the "body" of
whose "flesh" the "odious profaners committed
horrors and vengeance." (It should be noted,
however, that one of the leading British Biblical
scholars, Professor H. H. Rowley of Manchester
University, believes that "the language" here "seems
to favour" Dupont-Sommer's view.) In the case of
the other passage, Habakkuk 2:15, the words that
Dupont-Sommer translates, "Thou hast dared to
strip him of his clothing" may mean also "intended
him to go into exile" (Brownlee), "desired his
exile" (de Vaux). These points were immediately
made by Père de Vaux in *La Revue Biblique*, in a
review dated Jerusalem, March, 1951; and de
Vaux believes also that the words of the Commentary translated by Dupont-Sommer as "he
appeared to them all resplendent" do not imply a
transfiguration on the part of the Teacher of
Righteousness, but that the subject of the verb is
the Wicked Priest, and he shows that the verb
itself has also been found in a sense—that of merely
revealing oneself—quite remote from its original
meaning of causing oneself to shine.

It would seem that Dupont-Sommer has here
overplayed his hand. Yet the Teacher of Righteousness *was* persecuted, he does seem to have been
regarded as a Messiah; and the French scholar, in
his second volume, *Nouveaux Aperçus sur les Manuscrits
de la Mer Morte*, published in 1953 (and now trans-

lated as *The Jewish Sect of Qumrân and the Essenes*),
is able to support his thesis by pointing to the
following passage from *The Testaments of the Twelve
Patriarchs*, a late apocryphal work which has
already been mentioned above as connected with
the doctrine of the sect and fragments of which
have been found in the caves: "And now I have
learnt that for seventy weeks ye shall go astray, and
profane the priesthood, and pollute the sacrifices.
And ye shall make void the law, and set at nought
the words of the prophets by evil perverseness. And
ye shall persecute righteous men, and hate the
godly; the words of the faithful shall ye abhor.
[And a man who reneweth the law in the power of
the Most High, ye shall call a deceiver; and at last
ye shall rush (upon him) to slay him, not knowing
his dignity, taking innocent blood through wickedness upon your heads.] And your holy places shall
be laid waste even to the ground because of him.
And ye shall have no place that is clean; but ye
shall be among the Gentiles a curse and a dispersion
until he shall again visit you, and in pity shall
receive you [through faith and water]." When
R. H. Charles edited the *Testaments*, he regarded
this part of it as "unintelligible," and in his translation he put certain passages in brackets, as I
have left them in the extract above, in order to
indicate that he assumed them to be Christian
interpolations. But there is now no need thus to
exclude them, and the passage seems perfectly

appropriate if one applies it to the Teacher of Righteousness. The "Christos" of the Greek text, who figures also in other passages, is translated by Charles as "Christ"; but since "Christ" is merely the Greek for the Hebrew word "Messiah," both meaning "Anointed One," this does not imply that the references are not to the Teacher of Righteousness; and, if they are, it would appear that the Teacher did actually die at the hands of his enemies. *The Testaments of the Twelve Patriarchs* is, besides this, full of ideas and language that are similar, on the one hand, to the literature of the sect and, on the other, to that of Christianity. *The Two Ways* here turns up again; and Dr. Charles, writing forty years ago, clearly showed that "many passages of the Gospels exhibit traces" of the *Testaments*, and that "St. Paul seems to have used the book as a *vade mecum*." "There are over seventy words," it seems, "which are common to the *Testaments* and the Pauline Epistles, but which are not found in the rest of the New Testament." The most striking parallel, perhaps, is that between Matthew 25:35-36 and a passage from the Testament of Joseph I: 5-6. It is impossible to doubt that the former is an imitation of the latter or that both were derived from a common source.

I was sold into slavery, and the Lord of all
    made me free:
I was taken into captivity, and His strong
    hand succoured me.

I was beset with hunger, and the Lord Himself nourished me.

I was alone, and God comforted me:

I was sick, and the Lord visited me:

I was in prison, and my Lord showed favour
to me;

In bonds, and he released me. . . .

TESTAMENTS

For I was hungry and you gave me food,

I was thirsty and you gave me drink,

I was a stranger and you welcomed me,

I was naked and you clothed me,

I was sick and you visited me,

I was in prison, and you came to me. . . .

MATTHEW

And the promises of the Sermon on the Mount are
anticipated in several places: "And they who have
died in grief shall arise in joy; and they who were
poor for the Lord's sake shall be made rich; and
they who are put to death for the Lord's sake shall
awake to life." The gospel of forgiveness is all
through the *Testaments*; and there occurs here the
first known conjunction—which was to be repeated
in Mark 12:19-31—of the precept of Deuteronomy
6:5 to "love the Lord thy God with all thine
heart," etc., and that of Leviticus 19:18 to "love
thy neighbour as thyself." (The injunction to love
one's "neighbour" or "brother" turns up also in

*The Book of Jubilees* and the Zadokite fragments; and the great rabbi Hillel of the Talmud, who flourished in the first century B.C. and thus belongs to the same general period, is supposed to have said to a Gentile who had come to him and challenged him to convert him by teaching him the whole of the Torah during the time that he, the Gentile, could stand on one foot: "What is hateful to thee, do not unto thy fellow; this is the whole law." The conversation reported by Mark has a certain resemblance to this.)

Dr. Brownlee, in the paper already quoted, still maintained that though Dupont-Sommer had succeeded in his second book in "laying the foundation of his view somewhat more securely," he had "failed to bring it to rest safely upon incontrovertible proof texts." But he goes on to say that "Dupont-Sommer often has an uncanny knack for being ultimately right (or nearly so), even when his views are initially based on the wrong texts! So also in the present case there is a doctrine of a suffering Messiah in the scrolls, but not (so I believe) where Dupont-Sommer found it. This is found in a passage of the Manual of Discipline not then published, and in a passage not yet discussed in this connection." Now, one of the most impressive pieces of evidence that can be adduced from the Old Testament in support of the claim of the Christian that the advent of Jesus as Messiah had been prophesied in the ancient text is, of course, the chapter (53) of

Second Isaiah which speaks of a Suffering Servant, "despised and rejected of men, a man of sorrows," who has been "wounded for our transgressions," and yet by whose "stripes we are healed." If this is not Jesus, the Christians have asked, who can it possibly be? The scholars have proposed Israel, the unknown Second Isaiah himself, the real Isaiah and Jeremiah. None of these seems satisfactory; and Dupont-Sommer had suggested that Second Isaiah may date from a period as late as that which is dealt with in the literature of the sect. These later chapters of Isaiah had long been assigned to the Babylonian Exile, two hundred years later than the original Isaiah, and it had already been admitted that still later additions were possible. Why, now asks Dupont-Sommer, could these passages not have been written after the death of the Teacher of Righteousness? And "now that the alert has been sounded," he says, "many passages of the Old Testament must be examined with a fresh eye. Wherever it is more or less explicitly a question of an Anointed One or of a Prophet carried off by a violent death, how is it possible to avoid asking whether the person indicated is not precisely our Teacher of Righteousness?" He mentions certain passages from Daniel, Zechariah and Psalms; and he says of the passages in Second Isaiah called "Songs of the Servant of Yahweh," "For twenty centuries people have been asking who was this gentle and humble Prophet, this suffering righteous man whose agony has saved multitudes; the truth is that, apart from Jesus, the Christian Messiah, only one such is known in the whole of Jewish history—and this one has only been known for a very short time. It is the pious Master who was martyred by Aristobulus II. It is not a *single* revolution in the study of Biblical exegesis that the Dead Sea documents have brought about; they will mean, one begins to foresee, a whole torrent of revolutions."

It is impossible for the layman to estimate the value of this hypothesis. Let us simply return to Brownlee, who has been working, in connection with second Isaiah, on an interesting line of his own. What Brownlee calls "a startlingly new reading" of Isaiah 52:14 has been found in the complete Isaiah scroll discovered in the first cave. The addition in this text of a single letter changes the accepted meaning from "his appearance [that of the 'Servant'] was so marred beyond semblance," to "I so anointed his appearance beyond anyone (else)," and this for the first time makes plausible the beginning of the following verse, a passage over which editors have always stumbled. The new Revised Standard Version makes this, "So that he startled many nations," but the more obvious meaning of the verb would be, "so shall he *sprinkle* many nations" (it is so translated in the King James Version). But if the Suffering Servant of the Lord was *anointed* instead of *startled*, it would be natural that he should, in turn, have the mission of sprinkling the nations. Whoever was responsible for this variant, it seems plain that a definite Messiah is meant by the scribe of the Dead Sea scroll, and Dr. Brownlee, like Dupont-Sommer, associates this passage with the Messianic references in Zechariah and Daniel (9:24-27: the "Anointed One," who is to be "cut off"). Dr. Brownlee does not commit himself to the theory that this Messiah is the Teacher of Righteousness; but he does try to connect the *refining* and *sprinkling* referred to in the Manual of Discipline and associated with giving the adepts an "insight into the knowledge of the Most High," as well as the statement in the Manual that "God has chosen them to be an eternal covenant," with the language of Second Isaiah in the chapters on the Suffering Messiah. This would seem to make it probable that Jesus "intended to give his life [as] a ransom for many in fulfilment of Old Testament prophecy"—prophecy which, if it did not derive from, was cherished and elaborated in, the literature of the sect. It would appear, in other words, that Jesus may well have found prepared for him, by the teaching of the Dead Sea sect, a special Messianic role, the pattern of a martyr's career, which he accepted, to which he aspired.

When the Manual of Discipline was first discovered, the purgations by sprinkling that appear in it made the scholars at once think of John the Baptist, and there was even, at first, some idea that he might be the Teacher of Righteousness. John the Baptist is supposed to have been born—perhaps in Hebron—not very far away from the monastery; "the word of God" came to him, says Luke, "in the wilderness," which must have meant the bald and sub-sea-level mountains that stand between the monastery and civilization; and his ministry, according to Luke, was in "all the regions about the Jordan." He not only had the practice of baptism in common with the members of the sect, but he seems to be following their principles (Luke 3:11) when he preaches to "the multitudes" who have come to be baptized by him: "He who has two coats, let him share with him who has none; and he who has food, let him do likewise." Like the sect, he expects the Messiah, and like the sect—as Mr. Brownlee reminds us—he invokes, in this connection, the Second Isaiah: "The voice of one crying in the wilderness: Prepare the way of the Lord." But the sect lived together in this wilderness, whereas John, in the Gospels and Josephus, always appears as a lonely ascetic, like Bannus, the desert saint at whose feet Josephus had sat. What, then, was John the Baptist's relation to the sect? Dr. Brownlee suggests that John may have been one of those "other men's children" that Josephus says the Essenes adopted and "moulded in accordance with their own principles." "And the child grew," says Luke (1:80), "and became strong in spirit, and he was in the wilderness till the day of his

manifestation to Israel." This would give us an
explanation of the otherwise rather unaccountable
circumstance that John's childhood was spent in the
desert. I have nowhere seen it suggested that John
was at odds with the sect; but, in connection with
his desert diet of locusts and wild honey, one
remembers the expelled Essenes, who resorted to
living on grass because they had sworn an oath
never to eat any food not prepared by the brotherhood.

But what was the relation of Jesus to the ritual
and doctrine of the sect, which the Gospels so
persistently echo? Could he have been actually a
member of the sect during those early years of his
life when we know nothing about him—where he
was or how he occupied himself—or was his contact with it, as Albright believes, chiefly by way of
John the Baptist? We must remember that Bethlehem itself is not very far from the monastery. The
Bedouins were on their way there when they found
the scrolls in the cave. Now, John and Jesus,
according to Luke, were relatives on their mother's
side. Jesus, in his late twenties and hardly younger
than John, came down, we are told, from Galilee
in order to be baptized by John, and fasted forty
days in the wilderness. Not very long afterwards,
apparently, John was arrested by Herod, and then
the ministry of Jesus began. We know very little, of
course, about the first thirty years of Jesus' life—what
he had read or by whom he had been influenced.

We can feel behind the pages of his followers
the fire and dynamic force, the power to melt and
to magnetize, of an extraordinary personality. But
we know also that the rites and the precepts of the
Gospels and Epistles both are to be found on every
other page of the literature of the sect. Some
scholars believe, in the light of the scrolls, that the
Gospel according to John, which hitherto was
thought to have been written late and under the
influence of the movement—part Persian, part
Platonic—that goes by the name of Gnosticism,
must actually have come out of the sect and be the
most, instead of the least, Jewish of all the Gospels.
You have, at the very beginning of John, the
conflict between Light and Darkness, and thereafter
many such phrases as "the spirit of truth," "the
light of life," "walking in the darkness," "children
of light," and "eternal life," which occur in the
Manual of Discipline. And you have also, in the
Manual, a passage that parallels almost exactly the
description of the Logos ("Word") which stands
at the beginning of John and which has hitherto
been thought to derive from the Gnostics. Manual
11:11 reads, "And by his knowledge everything has
been brought into being. And everything that is, he
established by his purpose; and apart from him,
nothing is done." John 1:2-3: "He was in the
beginning with God; and all things were made
through him, and without him was not anything
made that was made."

What, finally, is the evolution that leads from
the morality of the sect—which imposes fraternal
forbearance among the members of the order
itself and which insists upon charity to the poor,
yet condemns and declares war on an enemy who
is trying to crush it—to the later morality of Jesus,
which is marked by occasional flashes of pugnacity
("I have come not to bring peace, but a sword")
yet is dominated by the principle of forgiveness?
How reconcile *The War of the Children of Light*, which
is full of soldierly weapons, with Philo's first-century
statement that the Essenes do not make weapons, or
its mention of animal sacrifices with Josephus's so
positive assertion that the Essenes had given these
up?

The answer is, no doubt, that we are dealing here
with the successive phases of a movement. Did the
return of the sect from its exile—which the earliest
of the coins of the second long sequence found by
de Vaux in the monastery seems to date about
4 B.C.—begin a new phase of its life, of which Jesus
and John, with their itinerant ministries, are somehow symptomatic or characteristic? One can, in
any case, plausibly explain the defiance of the
Teacher of Righteousness, the pacifism of Philo's
Essenes, and the turning of the other cheek of Jesus
as marking successive stages of the adjustment of
the Jews to defeat. We can see clearly in the Bible
how the Jewish God has been modulated from the
savage and revengeful Jehovah, who is feared and

propitiated in the Pentateuch, to the God of mercy and love who begins to be conceived by the later prophets. In *The Testaments of the Twelve Patriarchs*—assigned by Charles to the end of the second pre-Christian century—meekness and mercy are emphasized almost to the same degree that they are in the Gospels themselves. Is it that here the resentment of defeat is already giving way to resignation, the resignation of political helplessness; that neither Jews nor sectarians can hope to prevail, and that he who believes himself to be, or is believed by his followers to be, the desperately expected Messiah can preach only a moral salvation through faith in a non-militant God, and the righteousness of the individual? The sword that Jesus is bringing, in the quotation from Matthew (10:34) above, is the zeal for his own gospel, which will set the son against the father and make "a man's foes those of his own household." Yet in all this there seems still some conflict between, on the one hand, forgiveness and renunciation of the world and, on the other, combativeness and worldly ambition. In the language of the Sermon on the Mount there is what seems a strange vacillation between promising, on the one hand, to "the poor in spirit" "the kingdom of *heaven*," and, on the other, to "the meek" that "they shall inherit the *earth*." In the supposedly much earlier *Testaments*— in the passage already quoted, which seems obviously a prototype of the Sermon on the

Mount—the "poor" are to be made "rich."*

If, in any case, we look now at Jesus in the perspective supplied by the scrolls, we can trace a new continuity and, at last, get some sense of the drama that culminated in Christianity. We can see how the movement represented by the Essenes stood up for perhaps two centuries to the coercion of the Greeks and the Romans, and how it resisted not merely the methods of Rome but also the Roman ideals. We can guess how, about a half century before its refuge was burned together with the Temple of the Jewish God, this movement had inspired a leader who was to transcend both Judaism and Essenism, and whose followers would found a church that was to outlive the Roman Empire and ultimately be identified with Rome herself. Under the goading of these agonizing centuries, the spirit of the Essene brotherhood, even before its expulsion

* It should be mentioned that Dr. J. L. Teicher of Cambridge believes that the sect were Ebionites, "Poor Ones"—that is, Jews, who had been converted to Christ, but who continued Judaistic practices. The Teacher of Righteousness would then be Jesus, and the Man of Untruth, Paul, who has extended the cult to the Gentiles. One difficulty with the theory is that the dating of the departure from the monastery is too early to make this possible; and another that the literature of the sect contains no obvious mention of Jesus or any direct reference to his teaching. Dr. Teicher has tried to discover some, but the few resemblances he points to seem far-fetched or very faint. The words of Jesus should have left plainer marks on even still Judaizing adherents.

from its sunken base, had already thus made itself free to range through the whole ancient world, touching souls with that gospel of purity and light to which the brotherhood had consecrated itself, and teaching the contempt of those eagles which they had noted—with evident astonishment—that the army of their enemy worshipped. The monastery, this structure of stone that endures, between the bitter waters and precipitous cliffs, with its oven and its inkwells, its mill and its cesspool, its constellation of sacred fonts and the unadorned graves of its dead, is perhaps, more than Bethlehem or Nazareth, the cradle of Christianity.

One would like to see these problems discussed; and, in the meantime, one cannot but ask oneself whether the scholars who have been working on the scrolls—so many of whom have taken Christian orders or been trained in the rabbinical tradition —may not have been somewhat inhibited in dealing with such questions as these by their various religious commitments. It is surprising to the layman, and inspires respect, to find that the ablest of these scholars have been bringing to what a couple of centuries ago must have been for such men of the church almost a domain of pure myth, a keenness and a coolness that seem quite objective. On almost any aspect of the scrolls that demands special learning and special research you may find, by one of these churchmen, an acute and exhaustive study; and yet one feels a certain nervousness, a reluctance to take hold of the subject and to place it in historical perspective. On the Jewish side, as Habermann says, it is a fear of impairing the authority of the Masoretic text, and also, one gathers, a resistance to admitting that the religion of Jesus could have grown in an organic way, the product of a traceable sequence of pressures and inspirations, out of one branch of Judaism; on the Christian side, it is, of course, as Dr. Brownlee says, the fear "that the uniqueness of Christ is at stake," as well as a reciprocal resistance to admitting that the morality and mysticism of the Gospels may perfectly well be explained as the creation of several generations of Jews working by and for themselves, in their own religious tradition, and that one need not assume the miracle of a special magnanimous act of God to allow the salvation of the human race. Do these prejudices and preconceptions play some role in certain stubborn attempts—apparently, against all the evidence—of such scholars as Solomon Zeitlin of Dropsie College in Philadelphia and G. R. Driver of Oxford to date the scrolls very late? Dr. Zeitlin, who believes that the Karaites did not derive their doctrine from the Zadokites but wrote the Zadokite documents themselves, wants to put them in the eighth century. Dr. Driver inclines toward the sixth. In either case, their teachings could have played no role in the early development of Christianity. Do such considerations have anything to do with the persistence—not untinged, one fears, with acrimony—with which Dr. Joseph Reider, also of Dropsie College, has attempted to explain away the text of the Dead Sea Isaiah, in which W. H. Brownlee has found evidence of the Messianism either of Second Isaiah himself or of the scribe who made the Dead Sea copy?

New Testament scholars, it seems, have almost without exception boycotted the whole subject of the scrolls. The situation in this field is peculiar. It is precisely the more "liberal" scholars in Britain and the United States who have been most reluctant to deal with the scrolls, for the reason that these liberals tend to assume that the doctrines known as Christian were not really formulated till several generations after Jesus' death, and especially, as I have said, that the Gospel of John came late and was influenced by Gnostic thought. Professor Albright believes that the doctrine of John was "already either explicit or implicit before the Crucifixion," that the material relating to Jesus—though it was not written down till later—must go back to before 70 A.D. (by which date, according to the evidence of the coins, the Romans would have driven out the sect), and that it represents authentic memories and correctly reflects Jesus' teaching.

These new documents have thus loomed as a menace to a variety of rooted assumptions, from matters of tradition and dogma to hypotheses that are exploits of scholarship. How gingerly, in many quarters, the approach to the scrolls long remained has been shown in a striking way by the disturbing but air-clearing effects of the writings of Dupont-Sommer.

Professor A. Dupont-Sommer occupies a unique position in the controversy of the scrolls. I had noticed, in reading his books, that (so far as my experience went) he was the only one of all these scholars who invoked the authority of Renan. The author of the *Histoire du Peuple d'Israël* and the *Origines du Christianisme* calls attention to the first emergence in the "intertestamental" apocrypha of certain characteristic Christian themes, and M. Dupont-Sommer refers to this. I was, therefore, not surprised, when I met him, to find that he is conscious of carrying on what may be called the Renanian tradition. Renan now is *"vieux,"* he told me, in the sense that he now dates, but his ideal for writing history is valid. M. Dupont-Sommer himself occupies the chair of Hebrew at the Sorbonne, whereas Renan was professor at the Collège de France, but their roles are somewhat similar, and Dupont-Sommer is the present director of the project over which Renan presided and of which he sometimes said that he regarded it as the most important work of his life, the *Corpus Inscriptionum Semiticarum*. M. Dupont-Sommer, when one meets him, presents a remarkable example of a phenomenon encountered so often that it cannot be due wholly to coincidence. Just as biographers sometimes look like their subjects and ornithologists are often birdlike, so M. Dupont-Sommer in person astonishingly resembles Renan. He is round-faced, short and rotund, bland and urbane and smiling. This smoothness has perhaps a slight tinge of the priestly—for, as Renan first studied for the priesthood, so Dupont-Sommer was once an abbé. He is now, he says, "*un pur savant*," without any religious affiliations; and to an inquirer in the same situation, it is pleasant and reassuring to find that the great secular seekers for truth as well as the Teachers of Righteousness may establish their lasting disciplines. Such an inquirer comes finally to ask himself whether anyone but a secular scholar is really quite free to grapple with the problems of the Dead Sea discoveries. There may have been, perhaps, just a shade of the sensational in the manner in which Dupont-Sommer originally propounded his thesis in connection with the Habakkuk Commentary. Other scholars were certainly shocked, and a reference to the broken text will show, as I have said, that he has filled in the gap with a somewhat highhanded conjecture. Yet the fact, after all, remains that this independent French scholar has made so far the only attempt on any considerable scale to recover the lost chapter of history and to put it before the public. You can buy his two admirably written books—in the series *L'Orient Ancien Illustré*—at any first-rate bookstore in Paris. They have till now been the only source—aside from a few mostly perfunctory articles in newspapers and magazines—from which it was possible for the world at large to form any idea of the interest and scope of the writings contained in the scrolls. The whole subject, though the first announcements made news in 1948-49, has largely since been hidden from general knowledge in monographs and periodicals. In order to acquaint yourself, for example, with Dr. Brownlee's undoubtedly important ideas about the Suffering Servant of Isaiah, you must combine a technical paper of his on the language of the text in the *Bulletin of the American Schools of Oriental Research* with another paper by him which, chopped up into very short lengths, appeared in no less than five issues of the *United Presbyterian*, a church weekly published in Pittsburg. And it is impossible to explore this literature without becoming aware that the impact of Dupont-Sommer has not merely been to rouse resistance. It is evident that two of the ablest men who have concerned themselves with the scrolls—H. H. Rowley and Père de Vaux—in spite of their strong criticisms and their reservations, have in some respects been led to revise their views more nearly in conformity with his.

It must, however, be left to the scholars to criticize scholarly theories. The layman can but try to calculate whether a scholar committed to the Christian faith has anything really at stake in dealing with the possible debt of the morality and

practice of Christianity to those of the Dead Sea
sect. For anyone who believes that the Son of God
was born into the family of a carpenter of Nazareth
in northern Palestine, that he preached by the
Lake of Tiberias, and that he was questioned in
Jerusalem by Pilate, should it really be any more
difficult to admit that he had been trained in the
discipline and imbued with the thought of a certain
Jewish sect, and that he had learned from it the role
that he afterwards lived of teacher, Messiah and
martyr? Or will the explanation of Jesus—as well
as of Paul—in terms of pre-existent factors, the
placing him and visualizing him in a definite
historical setting, inevitably have the effect of
weakening the claims of divinity that have been
made for him by the Church? Anyone who goes
to the Gospels from the literature of the Dead Sea
sect must feel at once the special genius of Jesus and
be struck by the impossibility of falling in with one
of the worst tendencies of insensitive modern
scholarship and accounting for everything in the
Gospels in terms of analogies and precedents. The
writings of these pre-Christian prophets and saints
are often, though not always, insipid. Properly to
judge them, however, one would have to know them
in the Hebrew, which, in the case of the apocryphal
writings, has usually not survived; and one must
pay attention to General Yadin when he says of the
*Thanksgiving Hymns* that he "doubts that any
language other than the original Hebrew can

convey the depth of emotion and the spiritual beauty of these verses." Yet even in their non-classical Greek, the Gospels still convey an electrical power; they can move and excite and convert. I have spoken before of the moral audacity, the sense of spiritual freedom, that one gets from certain scenes in the Gospels; and such a passage of high drama as that of John 18-19: Jesus arraigned before Pilate, must surely have been inspired—like Plato's account of the trial and death of Socrates—(whether literally true or not) by a noble and commanding personality. Neither Hillel nor the author of the *Testaments* nor, apparently, the Teacher of Righteousness ever stirred and drew people as Jesus did. And yet, as Albright has said, it is now for the first time possible to "elucidate the New Testament historically in the light of the immediate background of John the Baptist and Jesus." Will or will not this process of elucidation inevitably have the effect of making Jesus seem less superhuman till he has come to appear miraculous only in the sense, say, that Shakespeare is miraculous: in relation to his predecessors? Professor Albright himself evidently does not think so, for he elsewhere declares that "the historian cannot control the details of Jesus' birth and resurrection and thus he has no right to pass judgment on their historicity. . . . The decision must be left to the Church and to the individual believer, who are historically warranted in accepting the whole of the Messianic framework of the Gospels or in regarding it as partly true literally and as partly true spiritually—which is far more important in the region of spirit with which the Christian faith must primarily deal."

Yes: only the believer can answer this. But, for one who is not concerned with the theological problem, the implications of the scrolls are reassuring. The point of fundamental importance was put to the present writer in a precise and conservative way by Professor Millar Burrows of Yale. "We now realize," he said, "that there was much more variety and flexibility in Judaism than had been supposed." To anyone who has given thought to the peculiar and strained relations that for centuries prevailed between Jews and Christians, and that in some quarters still continue, it must be plain that behind these antagonisms lies an ancient deep-seated fear on the part of each of these groups of the other. Almost everyone must have noted some instance of an involuntary irrational suspicion, in cases where it is quite unjustified, cropping up, if only for a moment, to trouble normal relations. I was told, when in Israel, an anecdote that is typical of this kind of situation. At the time of the last war, an Englishwoman in England had felt very strongly that enough was not being done for the Jewish refugees from Hitler. One of her neighbours in the country was Jewish, and one day when she was passing his house at the time he was watering his garden, she somehow got sprayed with his hose.

"Do you think he did it on purpose?," she appealed
to a Jewish friend. This reaction—the result of
instinctive fear combined with a feeling of guilt—
may be matched, from the other direction, by
instances in which Jewish critics have sometimes
found anti-Semitic implications in books where
there was certainly no question of anything of the
kind. This nervousness has recently been mainly
due to the atmosphere created by the Nazi persecutions; and these persecutions, of course, were not
carried on in the name of the ancient religious issues.
Hitler preached the innate inferiority of the Poles
as well as of the Jews, and he had repudiated
Christianity as a Jewish religion for mollycoddles;
the Nazi leaders, indubitably, in making a scape-
goat of the Jews, were playing on something in the
German mind so primitive as to seem pre-Christian.
Yet such persecutions could hardly have been
possible if there had not been the opportunity to
revive the traditional restrictions against Jews in
medieval Germany—restrictions which had been
the product of bigotry and superstition. The
Christians, brought up on the Gospels, have never
been able to forget that the Jews rejected Jesus and
demanded his death. For centuries—as I learn
from a Jewish historian, Dr. Cecil Roth—they could
not imagine that the Jews believed in good faith
that their Judaic theology, their ritual and their
law, were the true ones, given them by God through
Moses; the Christians were convinced that the

Jews knew better, and that their failure to accept
the Christian faith was due to a stubborn perversity
that must have the Devil behind it. It was for
centuries a Christian objective to convert the Jews
to Christ, and since they almost invariably failed
in this, the Christians became very bitter against
them. Even—as in Spain and Portugal—when they
extorted the forms of conversion, the Jews would
go on practising Judaism, and to the Christians it
seemed that their counter-religionists were still in
the same state of mind that had led them to crucify
Jesus, that they would willingly crucify him again.
This gave rise to the legend of the ritual murder of
Christian children at Passover, a symbolic perpetua-
tion of the Crucifixion. The reciprocal Jewish
legends connected with ritual murder—such as those
about Rabbi Loew of Prague—show that as late as
the sixteenth century the dwellers in the European
ghettos lived in continual terror of being framed for
this crime by the Christians: the great rabbi is
always rescuing them; and trials for ritual murder
were still occurring in Central Europe through the
turn of the nineteenth century. In the meantime,
the assumption of Jewish depravity had been giving
the followers of Christ carte blanche—not merely
with a quiet conscience but with fervour and
exaltation—to penalize, tax, torture and slaughter
the Jews, under the sign of the crucified Jesus.
On the Jewish side, the moral sense was outraged,
and the resentment to some extent still lingers, that

the communicants of a religion whose Deity is a God of Love and whose Saviour brings salvation through mercy, should, for example, inaugurate a crusade to the Holy Land for the purpose of rescuing the tomb of this Saviour by massacres of their Jewish compatriots. If the Christian has never ceased to be horrified by the callousness of the Jews toward Jesus, the Jew has never ceased to be shocked by what seems to him the hypocrisy of the Christians. A Jew, on occasion, in a position of power, may become as fanatical and ruthless as any other kind of man; but, though he may do it in the name of Justice, like certain of the Jewish Communists, he does not do it in the name of a religion which talks about forgiving everybody and turning the other cheek. Yet the bitterness of the Jew towards the Christian may have had other sources, too. I have sometimes imagined that the Jew has resented the success of Jesus, that he has been troubled by an uneasy sense that, in its day, the religion of Jesus was a beneficent, a "progressive" movement, and that the Christians have stolen his Messiah and attempted to appropriate his Bible. Of the two post-Christian Messiahs that have most raised the hopes of the Jews, one, Sabbatai Levi, let them down, under pressure, by confessing Muhammedanism, and the other, Jacob Frank, by succumbing to Christianity. The Orthodox Jew was left with a discipline of difficult observances, an anxious devotion to the letter of Scripture, which in time did perhaps as much as the malignity of Christian prejudice to keep him locked in his special compartment.

The rigours and repressions of this old Jewish world may be gauged by the attitude of the strongest spirits who have liberated themselves from it. I remember a conversation with the late Professor Morris Cohen—a man who gave the impression, as Mr. Alvin Johnson once said of him, of an alabaster lamp inside of which burned a bright flame. He told me—to my astonishment and rather to my horror—that, though he had loved the *Divine Comedy* in youth and had known a good deal of it by heart, he had never been able to bear it from the time that he broke with Judaism: it reminded him too claustrophobically of the tight medieval system in which he had himself grown up. As he talked, I became aware that this had actually distorted his conception of Dante, for whom Thomism was not really a prison, since he had his premonitions of the Renaissance and even some affinity with the Restoration. How close Morris Cohen remained, none the less, to this closed-in Orthodox world was shown me by a curious incident. In my then capacity as editor, sometime in the middle twenties, I persuaded him to write a short piece on a current documentary film that attempted an explanation of the Einstein theory. One day, some fifteen years later, I happened to meet him on a train. "You know," he said, "it was you who induced me to go to a movie—you paid me fifty dollars. It was the

only movie I have ever seen.' It was thus Morris
Cohen who gave me the first memorable glimpse
I had had of the conditions under which the Jewish
intellect had survived through the Middle Ages,
and I have had it in mind in the present connection.
It is as cramping to creative thought to accept the
Judaic restrictions as it is misleading and warping to
imagine that respect for suffering, consideration for
other people and the light of the Holy Spirit were
invented by Christianity. All these antiquated
prejudices and limitations sound crude enough when
thus stated baldly, but the present is hardly the
moment to take lightly the baleful power of fanatic-
isms and superstitions; and it would seem an
immense advantage for cultural and social inter-
course—that is, for civilization—that the rise of
Christianity should, at last, be generally understood
as simply an episode of human history rather than
propagated as dogma and divine revelation. The
study of the Dead Sea scrolls—with the direction
it is now taking—cannot fail, one would think, to
conduce to this.

In the meantime, it is going forward at what is
evidently a vigorous pace. In the handsome modern
museum in Old Jerusalem, built with Rockefeller
money, which has so admirably been designed to
fit into the architectural landscape of blunt yellow
towers and blank old walls, yet which makes you
feel, once inside, that you are luxuriously back in

New York, in a new wing of the Metropolitan, the fragments of the Dead Sea documents have been gathered and are being examined. Père de Vaux presides over this; and there are only three scholars authorized to decipher and report on the manuscripts: J. T. Milik, a Polish Roman Catholic priest; Dr. John Allegro of Manchester; and one American expert: last year Professor Cross of Chicago, at the present time Monsignor Patrick W. Skehan of the Catholic University of America. The tens of thousands of fragments—there has been no attempt to count them—have been put away in boxes. The utmost pains, of course, have been taken to keep separate the contents of the different caves and the pieces found in groups together. These range in size from morsels as large as your hand, which may include a whole column, to crumbs with a single letter. Some believe that it will take fifty years to sort them all out and decipher them, but the energetic de Vaux is more hopeful and thinks they may get through it in ten. The fragments selected for study are set out on long tables in a large white-walled room. They are mostly of leather but a few are papyrus. In colour, they range from the darkest brown to an almost paper-like paleness, so that they give the impression of autumn leaves that have lain in the forest all winter. The ones that are being studied have been flattened under plates of glass; but before they can thus be smoothed out, they have to be rendered less brittle by being put into a "humidifier," a bell-glass containing moist sponges. When they are taken out of this, they are cleaned with a camel's hair brush, dipped in alcohol or castor oil. Sometimes the ink comes off along with the marly clay of the caves. Sometimes they flake at the touch of the brush and have to be backed with tape. Sometimes they have turned quite black, in which case they are photographed with infra-red rays and examined through a magnifying glass. The first problem is to bring together—through a study of the various hands of the scribes and the substances on which they have written—the pieces that belong together. The scholars work on this in a small inner room, equipped with concordances, dictionaries and all the relevant texts. The concordance may place a fragment as coming from a Biblical book or a known non-canonical work, and others will be found to fit it.

The whole harvest of the fragments is not yet in; there are still hundreds in the hands of the Arabs, who have been making things more difficult by cutting the large pieces into strips and selling them one after the other at successive interviews—raising the price for the second piece, asking still more for the third, etc. To put a stop to this, it has been necessary to offer special baksheesh in proportion to the size of the pieces. It is estimated by Père de Vaux that fifteen thousand dollars is still needed to buy the rest of these fragments. It has been harder than one might suppose to raise the money required to purchase the mass of material that was carried away by the Arabs. A hard and fast rule has been made that the fragments must not be dispersed till everything has been classed and deciphered under Père de Vaux's supervision. Of course this is very wise: it is important to keep them together for comparison and co-ordination; but the effect has been somewhat to discourage institutions of learning from acquiring sets of these fragments, since any institution that buys them, as Manchester and McGill Universities have done, will not get them till they have already been read and published.

As one bends over the tables with the fragments under glass, one recognizes here and there—it is astonishing how beautifully clear much of the writing remains—the inextinguishable "tetragrammaton," the unutterable name of God. (The awe with which this name was treated is carried to a further remove in the Habakkuk Commentary, where it is written in archaic Hebrew—that is, in Phoenician—characters; and it should also be mentioned that fragments of various Biblical books among the later finds have added to the very few specimens known of manuscripts in Phoenician.) Here are most of the books of the Bible, though sometimes in an unfamiliar text or a text that corresponds with the Greek of the Septuagint but not with the Masoretic Hebrew; and there are also non-canonical books, unknown as well as known.

One wonders what new revelations may still come to light from these tatters. With what eagerness the scholars must hover over these layers of old leaf-mould spread out here!—an eagerness perhaps not unmixed, at moments, with apprehension.

The finds that, among these materials, are, I gather, causing most excitement, stimulating most expectation, are two as yet unread rolls of copper. Strips of copper like these, it seems, have hitherto not been known. They were found in one of the Qumrân caves that otherwise proved rather disappointing, one on top of the other, resting against the wall. It is supposed that they were hastily hidden there, and that access to the cave was soon afterwards made impossible by an earthquake. These copper strips have been rolled with the writing on the inner side, but the stylus has incised so deeply —it must have been pounded in—that the text can be partly made out in relief. The difficulty is to unroll these strips. They are green with oxidization and would crumble if subjected to pressure. Bits of them have been sent to Johns Hopkins in the hope of discovering some method by which they may be made more flexible. If this fails, they must be cut into sections. It has been calculated that, if put end to end, the two rolls would be eight feet long.

It was suggested at first that these strips were inscriptions from the walls of the monastery, and some have even imagined that they might come from the walls of the Temple, in which case they would have been taken down just before it was burned by the Romans in 70 A.D., and hidden away in a cave, about a mile and a quarter north of the monastery, when the monastery, too, was in danger. But Professor K. G. Kuhn of Göttingen, who has recently visited Jerusalem and studied the rolls in the museum, has come to a different conclusion. Deciphering as much of the text as can be read in reverse on the outside layers, he has found a succession of numerals accompanied by the word for cubits and a word that may mean either *buried* or a place—such as a ditch or a cave—in which something might be buried, as well as phrases such as "above," "on this side," "in the room," that seem to refer to locations. He believes that the strips are a list of the treasures of the monastery, with directions for finding the places in which they have been hidden from the Romans. They cannot, he thinks, have been plaques on the walls, since there are no signs of rivets or nails, nor does the text leave wide enough margins to make it possible that they may have been framed. One of the rolls consists of two separate pieces which can be seen to be fastened together, just as the strips of leather are in the scrolls, and this has led Dr. Kuhn to suppose that, like the scrolls themselves, they were meant to be unrolled and read. The members of the brotherhood, about to flee, would have written out their inventory on copper and put it in a cave by itself in the hope that it might survive, as leather scrolls might not do, the systematic wrecking of the Romans. If this turns out to be true, the archaeologists may have before them a veritable Gold-Bug treasure hunt.

# 6

## *General Yadin*

AND NOW let us return at last to the Metropolitan Samuel, who bought the first lot of scrolls and persisted in believing in their antiquity, who allowed them to be photographed by the scholars of the American School in Jerusalem and was encouraged by these Americans to come to the United States in January, 1949. The Metropolitan Samuel was hoping then to sell the scrolls to some institution of learning, but this turned out to be more difficult than the Americans had led him to believe. The publication of the texts by the School did not have the effect that had been predicted of exciting an interest in buying the manuscripts; on the contrary, it diminished their market value. Since the texts were available to scholars, there was no need to have the manuscripts in the library. The Metropolitan Samuel had signed an agreement that the

American School should publish within three years the texts that had been photographed, and that he should receive, in return, fifty per cent of the profits from the published texts. But the process of publishing Hebrew texts along with photographic facsimiles is a very expensive one. The first volume of the Dead Sea manuscripts cost the American School eight thousand dollars, and, though it has now gone into a second edition, it has been only in the last year that the Metropolitan Samuel has been able to collect any royalties: about three hundred dollars. Before this, the only revenue he was able to derive from the scrolls consisted of a few small fees that had been paid him for exhibitions in museums.

In the meantime, an outcry had been raised by the Department of Antiquities of Jordan, whose director is the British Harding, that the Metropolitan Samuel had had no right to take the scrolls out of the country, and that the Americans had no right to publish them and had connived with the Metropolitan in committing an illegal act. It was intimated that steps would be taken if he ever came back to Jerusalem. The American reply to this declares that it was precisely the men at the School who had explained to the Metropolitan the antiquity laws of Palestine, with which he was not familiar; that they themselves had reported the scrolls to the Department, and that, even before this, the Metropolitan himself, at the time he was looking for an expert opinion, had had them shown to the people of the Museum, and that in neither case had anybody connected with the Department exhibited the slightest interest;* and, finally, that when the Metropolitan at last took his scrolls abroad, his monastery was being bombarded by the crossfire of Jews and Arabs (the latter under the British Brigadier Glubb), and that, in the general chaos which the English had left, there was no safety for priest or manuscript, and no government, and hence no law, for antiquities or anything else. One recognizes at once in Jerusalem, whenever this subject is broached, the familiar Anglo-American feud that one has run into so often in Europe where the two nationalities have come together. The Yankees, the British imply, have as usual been guilty of sharp practice; the Americans retort that it was they, after all, who first realized the importance of the

---

* It should be noted that these statements have just been denied by Mr. G. Lankester Harding: "During the whole of this time [between the finding of the scrolls and the departure of the Metropolitan for America], if anyone seriously thought of reporting the matter to the Government Department of Antiquities the idea was apparently dismissed as sheer folly, for it was never done. The Archbishop's claim to have done so because he consulted a member of his flock who was assistant librarian at the Palestine Archaeological Museum can be discounted, as the person in question had no competence to give a judgment on antiquities of any kind, and even he did not report the matter to his superiors."—*Discoveries in the Judaean Desert. I.* Oxford University Press. 1955.

Metropolitan's manuscripts, and that they advised him to come to the United States in order to be sure of saving them. I might add, in support of the American side, that I was told by Professor Dupont-Sommer that European scholars are grateful to the men of the American School for so promptly making the texts available.

Dr. Burrows, of the Yale Divinity School, has been active in connection with the scrolls, and the Library of Yale University at one time considered acquiring the manuscripts, but finally decided not to. Those interested in the scrolls have complained —not without a certain justified bitterness—that the Library has had no difficulty in raising a sum that has been quoted at four hundred and fifty thousand dollars in order to buy the Boswell papers but could not produce the probably smaller sum that would have bought what were undoubtedly the most precious discoveries of their kind since the texts of the Greek and Latin classics brought to light in the Renaissance. This was all the more unfortunate because everything had not yet been published. There was a group of fragments of Daniel which the Metropolitan had not released, as well as a whole manuscript which had not even been read.

It was this manuscript, the smallest of his lot, that the Metropolitan had taken home with him, on the day of the photographing, when the layers turned out to be so stuck that it could not be easily unrolled. It has not been unrolled yet; but from

two fragments detached from the back, it has been
found to be written in Aramaic in "a very neat and
fine script." These pieces have been deciphered
by Dr. John C. Trever, who identified the word
BT'NWŠ with the feminine name Betenos in the
Ethiopic text of *The Book of Jubilees*. Betenos was the
wife of Lamech, one of the patriarchs in the early
part of Genesis, and the identification seems
established by a passage that reads, "then I,
Lamech, hastened to go in unto Betenos." Now,
in an ancient list of apocryphal works, a *Book of
Lamech* is mentioned, and it has been thought that
this must have been embedded in the later *Book of
Enoch*—Enoch was an ancestor of Lamech. But the
reading of the manuscript stopped there. The
Metropolitan took it to the Fogg Museum in
Cambridge, and the Museum authorities told him
that the scroll was gummed together by a gluey
substance like tar, which presented a problem in
organic chemistry. In view of the objections raised
by the Jordanians to the Metropolitan's title to the
scrolls, the museum insisted on insuring them against
possible suits on this ground, and the money to
cover the premium was found by Dr. C. H. Kraeling
of the Chicago Oriental Institute. The situation was,
of course, unusual, and since Lloyd's would not
undertake a policy, it was some time before the
Fogg was able to arrange for one. The Metropolitan
was asked, also, to sign a waiver that he would not
hold the museum responsible in the event of

damage to the scrolls. In the meantime, he had
taken them back, and he must have become
discouraged about getting the work done by the
Fogg, for he eventually dropped the whole matter.
He complains that whereas in the Middle East
arrangements are made by word of mouth and
usually lived up to by the parties, he has found that
in the United States you are always being asked to
sign papers, which turn out not to guarantee anything. He has, for example, always had to sign
agreements in connection with exhibiting his
scrolls, and he has made a point of stipulating that
no photographs of them should be taken. Such an
agreement was, however, violated when the scrolls
were shown in Chicago at the Oriental Institute.
A scholar who wanted to check on a disputed
passage managed to photograph a word that was
blurred, with infra-red rays. The Metropolitan
discovered this later when he came upon a learned
paper based on this photograph.

In the meantime, the scrolls were not sold, and
the scholars were becoming impatient and worrying
for fear the manuscripts might be deteriorating.
The Metropolitan, when he brought them to the
United States, had put them in a safety deposit
vault, and he had made them the charge of a trust,
the Trustees of which were Syrians of the Metropolitan's own church. All business connected with
them was to be transacted in the name of the trust,
the proceeds from selling them were to be handled

by it, and the money was to be devoted to church work and education. By this time, the Metropolitan had announced that he would not sell the Lamech roll separately. Since the value of the other manuscripts had fallen with their publication, he would now have less chance of disposing of them without the inducement of the unread scroll. He had decided to sell them in a lot, but not to set a definite price on them. He offered to have them appraised by experts. That he should have had to wait in vain for an American buyer throws into relief the false values of the market for rare books in this country. One remembers the one hundred and fifty thousand dollars paid by Dr. Rosenbach for a copy of the Bay Psalm Book, the one hundred and six thousand paid by him for a Gutenburg Bible, the fifty thousand for the first version of *Alice in Wonderland*. The difficulties about the Metropolitan's title may possibly have had something to do with the reluctance of learned institutions; but undoubtedly the principal obstacles were the relative poverty of such institutions—divinity schools and seminaries—as are interested in biblical manuscripts, and the high susceptibility of rich collectors, cultivated by the book dealers through decades, to first editions of classics that are perfectly accessible to everybody.

Last summer, General Yigael Yadin—the son of Professor Sukenik—visited the United States. He remained from the middle of May to the end of the first week in July. He and Albright discussed the scrolls, and Yadin then decided to try to raise the money from Israel. He wrote the Metropolitan a letter, to which he received no reply, and he concluded that it would not be possible for the Syrians, under the circumstances, to sell the scrolls openly to Israel. There was always the possibility that the Jordanians would appeal to the authorities and try to prevent them from leaving the country or that Jordan would bring a suit in the United Nations. The General's attention, however, was drawn to an advertisement in the *Wall Street Journal* that appeared during the first three days of June under the heading "Miscellaneous For Sale":

The Four Dead Sea Scrolls
Biblical Manuscripts dating back to at least
200 B.C. are for sale. This would be an ideal
gift to an educational or religious institution
by an individual or group.

The Syrians, becoming anxious, had resorted to this device. Yadin, without letting his name appear, applied to purchase the scrolls, using as intermediary a lawyer not associated with Israeli business, who negotiated the sale through a New York bank. The Syrians were never told that the manuscripts were going to Israel, and so ought to be held by the Jordanians quite innocent of selling them to their enemies. The price was two hundred and fifty thousand dollars. There happened to be a hundred thousand available in the treasury of an organization called the American Fund for Israeli Institutions, and Yadin persuaded his government to lend the remaining one hundred and fifty. An American millionaire in the paper business, Mr. D. Samuel Gottesman of New York, offered to repay the money to the fund and the Israeli government. The whole matter was kept a secret until the scrolls had been transported to Israel. This, of course, took place some time ago, but the purchase of the scrolls for Israel was not announced till February 13, 1955, when Premier Sharett explained that they would be housed, with other ancient documents, in a museum to be built for the purpose and to be called the Shrine of the Book. The first manuscripts found in the Qumrân cave are thus at last united in New Jerusalem. The Lamech scroll will now be opened, and the Hebrew University will publish its text. This will be of great interest to scholars, since it is the only known specimen of literary Aramaic from the period of four hundred years between the Aramaic of the Book of Daniel in the early third century B.C. and that of the Scroll of Fasting, a document of the second century A.D.

The Metropolitan Samuel has been living in Hackensack, New Jersey. There are in the United States four churches of his confession—one of them in West New York, not far away—and a single one in Canada. He has been travelling around among them, but his position has been rather difficult, for there has never been a metropolitan of the Syrian Jacobite Church in this part of the world before, and there is really no see for one. Exiled from the pomp and antiquity of his monastery in Old Jerusalem, he has taken a little cottage in a suburban section of Hackensack, where, supported by the Syrian congregation of the town, he has been living in modest comfort. I went to call on him there in the May of 1954. The white wood-work and neat brick of his new Colonial house stood out among the family residences, rather gloomy and sometimes shabby, of the older New Jersey suburbs. One crossed a small well-tended front lawn of glaring New Jersey grass to find his name and his rank, in the ancient Syrian lettering called estrangelo, spanning in wrought iron an ornamental glass outer door. He seemed an exotic figure with his dark and magnetic eyes, his Assyrian beard and enveloping robes, the sombre darkness of which was set off by a lining of brilliant puce. He told me that a good many of the Russian priests now in the United States have, except when officiating, discarded their priestly robes and taken to business suits, but that he has kept on wearing his. The furniture was modern American; two bookends had heads of Lincoln. But on the mantelpiece was a Syrian prayer book underneath a painting of Christ, and on one side of the fireplace hung a glowing ruby-studded crosier. He has made of this mantelpiece an altar, and he holds before it Sunday services for his Hackensack congregation. He was planning at that time to have built for himself a small cathedral in Hackensack.

I called on him again last February. I did not know that the scrolls had been sold. He greeted me with radiant good humour and explained that he had disposed of the manuscripts to a buyer who, for unknown reasons, would not allow his name to be revealed. The Metropolitan himself had seen only the vice-president of a bank. He entertained me with a sumptuous Syrian lunch of vegetables, salads, fruits and cheeses. The principal dish was fish, and the Metropolitan explained to me that in his Syrian Jacobite Church three days in February were appointed as a special Lent, to commemorate the fasting of the Ninevites when Jonah had preached to them and caused them to repent. This fast is a unique institution of the dissident Eastern churches. He told me that the money from the scrolls would be spent on education and church work for the Syrian Church in the Middle East. He was not clear, has perhaps not decided, what he himself will do now. There is no question, in any case, that he will somewhere be performing his archiepiscopal duties, untroubled by the controversies provoked by the scrolls.